Succe...
Interna...
COMMUNICATION

Understand and enhance your communication skills

A
Awareness

D
Don't Judge

A
Analyse

P
Persuade Yourself

T
Try

CHIA SUAN CHONG

Pavilion

Successful International Communication

Published by:
Pavilion Publishing and Media Ltd
Rayford House
School Road
Hove
East Sussex
BN3 5HX

Tel: 01273 434 943
Fax: 01273 227 308
Email: info@pavpub.com

Published 2018

ISBN: 978-1-912755-13-4

Pavilion is the leading training and development provider and publisher in the health, social care and allied fields, providing a range of innovative training solutions underpinned by sound research and professional values. We aim to put our customers first, through excellent customer service and value.

Author: Chia Suan Chong
Content editor: Ian McMaster
Editor/Publisher: Kirsten Holt, Pavilion Publishing and Media Ltd.
Production editor: Mike Benge, Pavilion Publishing and Media Ltd.
Content editor: Ian McMaster
Cover design: Phil Morash, Pavilion Publishing and Media Ltd.
Page layout and typesetting: Anthony Pitt, Pavilion Publishing and Media Ltd.
Printing: CMP Digital Print Solutions

Contents

For Mike: my inspiration, my soulmate, and my rock.

Introduction

Who am I?

I often struggle when people ask me where I am from. I was born in Singapore, a small multi-cultural society where I grew up amongst people from different backgrounds. In my teens, I spent nearly all my school holidays in Japan living with a family. While pursuing a career as an actor in my early twenties I moved to London, where I grew into an adult and gradually discovered who I was, what I valued and what I believed in.

It was in this capital city that I began teaching students from all around the world, where I did my Masters in Applied Linguistics, and where I found my career in writing and communication skills training. To me, London is as much a home to me as Singapore was, and during my 13 years of living there, I never hesitated to answer the question, 'Where are you from?' with the answer, 'London'.

After a year living in Munich, where I married Mike (who, incidentally, is Irish but who had lived in Germany for 15 years), we had our first child and I moved my multi-cultural family to York, a city in the north of England. Here I began another chapter of my life; taking on the role of a mother, becoming fast friends with other mums and embracing family life. One could say that my identity is an amalgamation of my experiences in life, the different people that I've spent time with, and the different cities and countries I've lived in.

I refer to myself as British, but also as Singaporean. When I talk about my ethnicity, I talk about being Chinese, although I've never been to China. I can't live without rice and Chinese food; I love all things Japanese; I feel indebted to the very effective German healthcare system; my heart burst with pride when London hosted the Olympics; I ran around the room cheering at the top of my voice when England scored six goals in a World Cup match; and I couldn't stop beaming when York was voted as best place in the United Kingdom to live.

I feel a sense of solidarity with the different communities that have accepted me. And while I sometimes feel displaced, I also feel like a global citizen fortunate enough to have had the encounters that have made me who I am today.

And in this age of globalisation and transnational mobility, I know I am not alone in this. Even those who have never contemplated moving away from their place of birth are coming into contact with people from different nationalities and different backgrounds through work, education, travel and immigration. Businesses are inevitably engaged in international dealings in order to cut costs, tap into new markets and expand their horizons. International project teams are becoming the norm in multi-national companies.

When communicating internationally, we might speak the same language but many of us still see the world through our own filters, applying the rules and norms that we are used to. We struggle when faced with different behaviours and practices, and sometimes find it hard to withhold judgment of ways that seem different from our own.

But we humans are also flexible creatures. With the right frameworks and the opportunities to reflect, we can gain an awareness that can change the way we relate to and communicate with people who seem – and may well be – different from us.

And this is what this book intends to try and do. From the experiences I've gained, the people I've met, the trainees I've helped and the observations I've made, I have put together anecdotes, case studies and critical incidents (see below) that encourage thoughts and reflections of personal experience to increase awareness which in turn will foster a better understanding of the issues underlying international communication.

In addition to supplying handy frameworks, tasks and communication tips, this book aims to explore the different areas of international communication, and provide useful support and guidance to anyone who finds themselves in a situation where they have to communicate with someone who might communicate in a different way from themselves.

How this book is organised

The book is divided into ten chapters, the first two of which provide a background to the topic of international communication. The rest of the book contains eight chapters on the key skills we need for communicating internationally.

- **Chapter 1** looks at the phenomenon of English as today's global lingua franca and how English is used as a tool for communicating internationally, by both native and non-native speakers of the language.

- **Chapter 2** explores intercultural awareness by looking at the definition of culture, the existing cultural frameworks and the factors influencing one's intercultural competence. In this section I also introduce the ADAPT model, a framework I use to encourage reflection and flexibility when communicating internationally.

- **Chapters 3–10** go on to look at the specific communication skills essential for international communication: from how we build relationships and make small talk (Chapter 3) to how we listen (Chapter 6), how we give and receive feedback (Chapter 7), how we persuade and influence people (Chapter 8) and how we deal with conflict (Chapter 9).

Most of this book does not have to be read in chronological order and you can dip in and out of the different chapters depending on what is most relevant or interesting to you. However, I do suggest that you read chapters 1 and 2 first, so as to gain a better understanding of the full picture.

Key features

Critical incidents

In this book, you'll find many anecdotes and critical incidents. A critical incident is a communication situation that one or more participants find problematic or confusing. Commonly used in management and in intercultural studies as an exploratory investigative tool, the Critical Incident Technique was originally defined by psychologist John Flanagan[1] as, 'a set of procedures for collecting direct observations of human behaviour in such a way as to facilitate their potential usefulness in solving practical problems and developing broader psychological principles'.

---

1   Flanagan JC (1954) The critical incident technique. *Psychological Bulletin* **51** (4) pp327–358.

Critical incidents provide us with a way of experiencing a situation we might be unfamiliar with, and give us the opportunity to think carefully and analytically about the behaviours that contribute to the success or failure of the situation. In doing so, they can help us develop the ability to see things from different perspectives.

The anecdotes, cases and critical incidents you will find in this book are not fictional. They are based on or inspired by real-life incidents that have happened to myself, my friends, and my clients and trainees. However, the names and sometimes the places, have been changed so as to protect the identities of the people involved, but I do so without changing the essence of the incident.

Tasks

This book contains multiple tasks to encourage thought and reflection. You can choose to do the tasks on your own, or with a partner. Sometimes, having someone to do these tasks with can trigger interesting discussions and revelations.

In order to signal tasks that often require a moment of reflection, you will see this icon:	
There is often a debrief after a task or a critical incident, where I will explore what has happened and/or consider the learning points of the task. Here, you will see this icon:	
This book also contains several useful lists and top tips that will come in handy when communicating internationally. Here, you will see this icon:	

While reading this book, you might find that some of the anecdotes remind you of situations you've encountered in the past, or you might gain a new perspective on something you've experienced before. You might have strong opinions on certain issues or you might find out about techniques and strategies that you've never tried. Consider writing these thoughts down as you go along as they can act as a powerful catalyst for your own reflection.

I sincerely hope that you will enjoy reading this book and find it useful in your international encounters.

Acknowledgements

I would like to thank the following people: Ian McMaster for his editorial support; Kirsten Holt and the team at Pavilion Publishing for their support and for making this possible; Emma Grisewood for kicking this off; Lauren Watson, Dawn Forrester and Mike Hogan for reading my book and being part of my initial test group; my friends, trainees and students who have spurred moments of reflection in me and have contributed both directly and indirectly to the critical incidents in this book; my clients and workshop participants who have trialled the tasks and critical incidents with me and given me valuable feedback; my mother- and father-in-law, Kathleen and Chris Hogan who are always ever so supportive of my work and my writing; my dad Francis Chong for teaching me to think critically from a young age, and my biggest loves: Isabelle, Natalie and Cillian, who have patiently tolerated me as I juggle my work and my family life.

Chapter 1: English as a lingua franca

What is English as a lingua franca (ELF)?

Growing up in Singapore in the 1970s and 80s, I encountered people with very diverse relationships to the English language. As an ex-British colony, Singapore chose to keep English as one of its four official languages (alongside Malay, Mandarin Chinese and Tamil) and as its main language of administration and international business when it gained independence in 1965. English was the medium of instruction at school and served as a *lingua franca*[2] that enabled Singapore's diverse population to communicate and interact with one another.

When I was at school, some of the other students spoke English and Mandarin to almost equal proportions both at home and at school, some had a Chinese dialect (e.g. Cantonese or Teochew) as their home language and reserved English for their friends at school, and others were more comfortable speaking exclusively in English wherever they were. I had friends who I spoke to in English peppered with Chinese and Malay words, but I also had friends who would interact with me predominantly in Mandarin peppered with English words or Singlish[3] expressions. I spoke Singaporean English (which followed the rules of British English but with a Singaporean pronunciation) and I spoke Singlish, and I would switch between the two quite comfortably, depending on whom I spoke to.

Language was thus a tool for us to connect and bond with each other, and although the Singaporean government and the teachers at school preferred us to stick to standard Singaporean English, we sometimes would accentuate our Singlish to make a point, to create humour, to exaggerate or be dramatic, or to establish solidarity. When asked, many Singaporeans would undoubtedly say that English is their native language and a huge part of their identity, but so

---

2 A common/vehicular language used to make communication possible between people who do not share a native language.

3 Often considered an English-based creole, with its own grammar rules and pronunciation.

is Singlish. Our ability to manipulate the English language has enabled us to nurture and showcase the different aspects of our identity and has helped us to adapt and accommodate the different conversation partners that we encounter.

In Singapore, English serves as a common language between Singaporeans with different mother tongues and is an intra-national lingua franca. Not too unlike the Singapore scenario, but on a much more global scale, English now serves as an international lingua franca: a tool to facilitate international communication between those who have English as one of the common languages that they choose to communicate in. People involved in education, trade, tourism or research, those participating in international business teams and negotiations across borders, and individuals employed by multi-national corporations might find themselves needing to use English in order to share information, manage relationships, and get things done.

So, how many people around the world are there using English? According to David Crystal[4], 375 million people speak it as their first language, but of the world's approximate 7.5 billion population, one in four of them speak it as a second/foreign language. With the number of so-called non-native speakers far exceeding the number of native speakers, it is hardly surprising that many non-native speakers are using English to communicate with other non-native speakers[5]. (The terms *native speaker* and *non-native speaker* themselves are problematic ➜ see *Who owns English* on page 13 for more details.)

Several years ago I was shopping in a well-known global retail chain store in Berlin when I overheard two Spanish-speaking managers instructing the German employees of the store in the basics of product display and customer service. A mixture of Spanish and English was used when the two Spanish managers were communicating between themselves, a mixture of German and English was used amongst the German employees, but when the Spanish managers were communicating with the Germans in that store, English was clearly the preferred medium.

While there used to be a time when people learnt English as a foreign language in order to travel to England or America and assimilate in the local culture, the reality of globalisation means that many are now learning English to get better jobs in multinational companies; become competent enough to

---

4 Crystal D (2012) English as a Global Language (2nd edn). Cambridge: Cambridge University Press.

5 Seidlhofer B (2004) Research Perspectives on Teaching English as a Lingua Franca. *Annual Review of Applied Linguistics* 24 pp209–239.

take on responsibilities that require international communication; or to get into their local universities, some of which now have English as a medium of instruction. The learning of English is no longer connected to learning about British culture: the royal family, fish and chips, Shakespeare or Byron. Neither is it a must for those learning English to learn about Christmas and Thanksgiving, George Washington and Abraham Lincoln, and the different states of America. The English language can exist as a separate entity from the history, the traditions and the practices of so-called native speaker countries like the United Kingdom and the United States, and used as a neutral tool of communication between two speakers who might not share a first language.

Who owns English?

A Filipino friend of mine, Bill, was attending a brainstorming meeting with some British colleagues. When asked for an adjective to describe a particular scene, Bill offered the word *picturesque*. One of his British colleagues, Paul, turned to him and growled, *'That's not a word'*. When Bill insisted that such a word existed, Paul snapped and said, *'Stop making words up. That's not an English word. I'm English, so I should know'*.

We might laugh at Paul's lack of vocabulary knowledge, or his ignorance, but his attitude towards Bill was due to the fact that he felt a strong ownership of the English language, and since Bill wasn't English, Paul felt that Bill did not have the right to challenge his knowledge or to *make up words*. However, Bill also felt a strong ownership of the English language. Bill grew up with both English and Tagalog, writes his journal entries and social media posts in English, and works in English. While Bill is multilingual, English is his main language and a huge part of his identity. So despite Paul's nationality and his perceived birthright, Bill felt an equal right to owning the language, albeit in his own way.

The example above might be an extreme one, but it is not uncommon for some native-speakers of English to feel that it is their language that is being appropriated and misused by the rest of the world. In 1995, the Prince of Wales was reported by *The Times*[6] to have criticised the Americans for inventing all sorts of nouns and verbs and making up words that shouldn't be, thereby corrupting the English language. But speak to any American, and they are likely to feel that English is very much their language, with the British sounding strange and old-fashioned.

---

6 24 March 1995. Quoted in Jenkins J (2003) *World Englishes: A resource book for students*, Oxon: Routledge, pp 4–5.

After all, language change is inevitable and has been happening throughout the ages. While we bemoan our younger generation's use of chat-speak and emojis, others have criticised the evolving nature of the language and, for example, rejected the use of a phrase like 'to send a meeting *invite*', insisting instead on 'a meeting *invitation*'. Previous generations complained when the verb *edit* was brought into use as a derivation from the noun *edition*, and over the centuries, words like *thy, thou, thee* and *thine* have simply been replaced by *you*. Most attempts to circumnavigate changes have been futile as language is ultimately alive and malleable in the hands of those who use it for their purposes. Meanwhile, new words like *binge-watch, emoticon, staycation* and *glamping* have all found their way into official English dictionaries.

However, the 'right' to play with language, use it flexibly and invent new words often seems to lie with the native speakers. At a restaurant one day, a group of friends were trying to decide on their drinks order when the East-Asian lady in the group asked her friends if they were *beer-ing* it or *wine-ing* it. She had previously heard her native-speaker friends ask if they were *bus-ing* it or *train-ing* it when they were making their way to the restaurant. Being an expert user of English, she decided to creatively coin new verbs to describe their choice of beer or wine. One of her friends turned to her and sympathetically advised, '*You can't say that. Those aren't English words. You have to say, "Are you having beer or wine?"*' When is a creative usage of a word referred to as artistic license and creative freedom and when is it a mistake? Might it be connected with the *native-ness* of the speaker?

The terms *native* and *non-native* themselves are fraught with problems. What qualifies Paul and not Bill as a native speaker? And if Bill is not a native speaker of English (when English is his main language), then what is he a native speaker of?

 Consider the following cases. In your eyes, which of them are native speakers of English? Why?

Marc was born in Japan to an American father and a Japanese mother. English is his predominant home language but Japanese was the language of his school and of Marc's social life.

Olga was born in Britain to Portuguese-speaking parents. Portuguese was her home language until she began going to school in England. English then became mixed in with Portuguese when Olga spoke to her parents, and when speaking to her siblings, it's always in English.

Michael was born in New Delhi to British expat parents. He attended the local school where Indian English was the medium of instruction and he also studied Hindi. He spent the first 16 years of his life in New Delhi, speaking English at home, and a mixture of English and Hindi to his friends, before moving back to Britain.

Sophia was born in Switzerland to a Korean mother and a Greek father. Her home language has always been English as it is the language her parents use to communicate with each other. She understands Korean and Greek but can't speak it fluently. She was educated in English and German at school, but also speaks French fluently.

Vicky was born and raised in Argentina where she spoke Spanish both at home and at school. When she was 16, she moved to Canada, where she went to an English-speaking university. She went on to become a professor at that university where all her written and spoken communication is in English. She sometimes worries that she might have forgotten her Spanish.

Looking at your responses to the above cases, were you able to come up with a satisfactory definition for the term *native speaker?* Some dictionaries define a *native speaker* as someone who learnt to speak a language from earliest childhood. The language in question is usually the language their parents speak and/or the language of their country of origin. But, in the very global communities we live in today, there is the likelihood that the languages spoken at home might differ from the languages spoken in their local communities, which might again differ from the languages they become confident at using in later life.

Even if we do manage the tricky task of defining a *native-speaker*, amongst them are numerous varieties of English, each with their own unique pronunciation features, colloquialisms and idioms. In Britain alone we have Mancunian English from Manchester, Scouse from Liverpool, Geordie from Newcastle, Black Country from the West Midlands and Cockney from London, to name just a few. Although R.P. (Received Pronunciation) was considered the *standard* prestigious accent, and the *Queen's English* was deemed to be the benchmark of *correct English*, users of more regional varieties of English take pride in *their English*, seeing it as a marker of their identity. National institutions like the BBC, which used to exclusively feature R.P. accents, have now increased the number of regional accents featured on their radio and television channels.

Amongst those who speak English as a foreign language too are local versions of English with their unique pronunciation features and English words adapted for or blended with their local language. For example, saying someone likes *skinship* (*skin + relationship*) in Korean English means that they like being tactile with their friends. Labels like *Chinglish* (Chinese English), *Spanglish* (Spanish English), and *Danglish* (Danish English) were coined to help describe the phenomenon at hand.

Professor Kurt Kohn of Tubingen University spent years exploring how English learners go about making English their own. Although teachers of their English classes might offer a model akin to a native speaker variety such as British English, learners very rarely acquire what is taught wholesale. In a speech Kohn gave in the 2012 TESOL Convention, he emphatically asserts, '*Learners never speak like their teachers!*'[1]

The input from their classes is inevitably synthesised with their social interactions, the other languages they speak, their goals and ambitions, and their language learning experience, all of which come together to help construct and create their own version of English, which Kohn calls *My English*. This English becomes an expression of their individual and social identity. While some learners might feel compelled to imitate the *native speaker* model, others might be more comfortable developing their own style and making English authentic for themselves, and in the process taking ownership of the language.

When it comes to ownership, the English language could be compared to football. The sport might have originated in England, but today people from all over the world play it. Some are expert players and some are just learning to play. Some play it professionally and some for fun. Some are good at defending and some at attacking. Some use it as a tool for improving their fitness and others a way to impress others. Everyone has their own style and everyone loves it in their own way. And no one would ever say that the English own football and so have more right to it than others. The same should apply to the English language.

So who owns English? Ultimately, I'd like to think no one and everyone.

---

1   https://www.youtube.com/watch?reload=9&v=yCfpD49YhSg

ELF and intelligible communication

So if everyone has their own version of English, how will they be intelligible to the rest of the English-speaking world? Far from being a static construct, an individual's English is constantly being shaped by their experiences with the English language and their relationship with it, and might change depending on the people they use English with and the context they're in.

Sean, for example, was born and raised in Glasgow and speaks only English. He works in London but maintains his Glaswegian accent because he's proud of being Glaswegian, although he finds himself shifting his pronunciation slightly in order to be understood easily by his colleagues. When he heads home to Glasgow for a visit, his Glaswegian accent is strengthened, and he uses Glaswegian colloquialisms as a way of bonding with his friends.

However, Sean does a lot of his business with the Chinese, the Thai and the Indians, and he finds it helpful to avoid dropping certain sounds (like the 't' in *water*) and to speak clearly, albeit with a Glaswegian intonation when communicating internationally. This ability to adapt has not made Sean less Glaswegian, and it is in fact this ability to manipulate the language at will, using it and changing it to best suit his different purposes, that makes him an effective communicator.

Unfortunately, many English-speaking monolinguals do not enjoy the successes of communication that Sean does. In ELF research, academics often refer to this familiar anecdote: a multinational group of people are sitting together for a meeting. Although English is their second or third language, they seem to understand what each other is saying. Then an English-speaking monolingual walks into the room and starts chatting away. Everyone looks at each other and no one seems to understand him/her.

And it's not only the academics and the English teachers that are discussing this issue. Successful English businessman and billionaire Sir Alan Sugar has recognised the necessity to use what he calls *Trade English* in order to succeed in international business[7]. We need to adapt the English we use as native speakers to the different international contexts we find ourselves in or risk losing potential business.

---

7 Sir Alan Sugar said this in the boardroom of The Apprentice UK, Series 6, Episode 8, in reaction to candidate Laura's inappropriate use of English with a German client. See: https://www.youtube.com/watch?v=_mw2ERDHyfQ

In recent years, numerous articles have been written (e.g. by the BBC and the Telegraph) about how the native speaker is a major contributor to breakdowns in international communication. Clearly, simply having a high level of proficiency and fluency is not enough to be intelligible. Some of the issues English-speaking monolinguals seem to have with international intelligibility include fast speech, strong accents, the use of extremely localised idioms and colloquialisms, cultural references and obscure words and phrases, and a lower tolerance of other varieties and uses of English.

However, there is a common misunderstanding that using English as a lingua franca is equivalent to dumbing down your English and simplifying it to the point of being grammatically incorrect. Concepts like *Globish*[8] (that uses a vocabulary list of 1,500 English words) and *Basic English*[9] (that uses a 850-word core words list) make use of a subset of English grammar and a reduced vocabulary which doesn't paint a clear picture of the complexity of international communication and leads people to wrongly assume that simplification is the key to using English in the global arena.

10 top tips for successful communication

So, how can proficient English users and native speakers use language more effectively when speaking to non-native speakers? Here are my top ten tips for expert users of English using English in international communication:

❶ Speak clearly

Unlike conversations in a movie script, real life conversations are often peppered with interruptions, false starts, repetitions, awkward silences, markers like *well, you know, okay, oh, yeah*, utterances that end trailing in mid-sentence, and references to what is (sometimes wrongly) assumed common knowledge. These features could potentially make mutual understanding complicated, especially for those who are communicating in a foreign language.

When communicating internationally, try to:

- Avoid mumbling.
- Be very clear in your mind what it is you want to say before speaking. Think about what your key message might be. This would reduce the unnecessary *white noise* that might be clouding the significance of what you are saying.

---

8   Jean-Paul Nerriere, http://www.globish.com
9   Charles Kay Ogden https://en.wikipedia.org/wiki/Basic_English

- Don't let your sentences trail off with the expectation that people know what you mean and therefore you don't need to say it. They probably don't know what you mean and you DO need to say it.

❷ Slow down

Some people are naturally fast talkers and some find their speed of speech increases when they are nervous or excited. Fast speech often also means that words are swallowed or mumbled and points are made in quick succession, not allowing the listener any time to think and respond to what is being said.

When communicating internationally, try to:

- Watch your speed of speech. Don't just slow down temporarily. Stay slowed down.

- Record yourself speaking and listening to the recording when you have a quiet moment to reflect. You might not realise that you talk as quickly as you do.

- Speak each word like you mean it. 'Own your words and enunciate them!' as stage actors often say.

❸ Be aware of the language you use

Are you overcomplicating the language that you use? Sometimes when using a language that you are so familiar with, it's hard to be aware of what is more easily understood and what might be less intelligible.

Consider the following cases. In your eyes, which of them are native speakers of English? Why?

A. (i) Should you happen to see him, would you mind letting him know that I'm expecting him to hand in the report soon as?
(ii) If you see him, please tell him to give the report to me as soon as possible.

B. (i) How are you keeping yourself occupied this weekend?
(ii) What are you doing this weekend?

C. (i) How do you make a living?
(ii) What job do you do?

D. (i) He was caught between the devil and the deep blue sea.
(ii) He was stuck between two bad choices.

E. (i) Gary was flat busted/Gary didn't have a nickel to his name.
(ii) Gary didn't have any money.

> In each example, the first options (i) offer a more verbose and more complicated way of saying something, thus increasing the possibility for miscommunication. Consider what is to be gained by using option (i) instead of (ii). Complicated grammatical patterns like *Should you happen to...*, trendy native speaker talk like *soon as* (instead of *as soon as possible*), highly-localised idioms like *flat-busted* or more archaic idioms like *didn't have a nickel to his name*, can all serve to create awkward situations of non-understanding.

When communicating internationally, try to:

- Think about the language you choose to use. Is it over-complicated? Does it contain colloquialisms and slang words? Could it be interpreted in more than one way?

- Consider if the idiom you wish to use might be only understandable to the people who live in your region, e.g. *Gary is flat-busted*.

- Consider if there is a more internationally understood idiom or expression you could use, e.g. *Gary is broke*.

- Consider if there are more straightforward ways of saying what you want to say, e.g. *Gary doesn't have any money*.

- If you must use an idiom but suspect it might be obscure, explain yourself. You could say, '*He was stuck between two bad choices. Where I come from, we would say, "He was caught between the devil and the deep blue sea".*'

- Ensure that what you say is a result of a choice you've consciously made, and not a result of a lack of awareness.

❹ Avoid too many cultural references

If you are used to only speaking to people from your local community, you might not be aware of the number of cultural references made during your everyday conversation. You might refer to pop icons and celebrities, political figures, historical events, news events, places in your country, TV shows or music (past and present), groups of people in your country (e.g. *Hipsters, Essex boys, Valley girls*), etc. References to such topics can generate conversations and help people bond, as long as they are familiar references to those involved in conversation.

When communicating internationally, try to:

- Be aware when choosing to make a cultural reference and realise that you might need to explain it to your conversation partner.

- Understand that too many unfamiliar cultural references can lead to confusion and might kill a conversation.
- Be mindful when talking in a group. While one or two of your conversation partners might understand your cultural references, this might exclude those who don't follow what you are saying.

❺ Use humour carefully

Humour is often used to break the ice, to ease the tension and to bond with others. However, it can also exclude and confuse. A search for the top 100 jokes on the internet would immediately reveal a list of jokes that feature a play on words. Some of them would require some cultural knowledge, like this one: *'Doc, I can't stop singing The Green, Green Grass of Home.' He said: 'That sounds like Tom Jones syndrome.' 'Is it common?' I asked. 'It's not unusual', he replied.*

For those unfamiliar with the Welsh singer Tom Jones and his hits *The Green Green Grass of Home* and *It's Not Unusual* would struggle to understand the joke. It is not surprising that our cultural upbringing has a lot to do with our sense of humour.

When communicating internationally, try to:

- Avoid making jokes that feature a play on words
- Avoid jokes that might require cultural knowledge to decipher.

(For more on humour, → see Chapter 3.)

❻ Listen actively

Sometimes when you are the more proficient speaker in an interaction it is easy to end up dominating the conversation. However, effective international communication is about listening as much as it is about speaking. If your conversation partner is less proficient in their ability to converse, your ability to listen actively can help boost their confidence immensely. (→See Chapter 6 for more on active listening.)

When communicating internationally, try to:

- Give others the opportunity to speak. Ask for their opinions.
- When others are speaking, support them by showing that you are listening and asking relevant questions.
- Be patient. Avoid interrupting and allow the speaker thinking time and time to finish what they are trying to say.
- Try to involve everyone. When there is more than one proficient English speaker in the group, it can be easy to neglect the less confident speakers.

❼ Ask for clarification

When we are in a conversation, we might sometimes encounter situations where we fail to understand something someone is saying. We might then choose to (i) let it pass and not talk about it, (ii) ask our conversation partner to repeat what they said, and if we still didn't understand it, then we let it pass and pretend that we got it, (iii) ask for clarification. We might choose to do (i) and (ii) perhaps because we feel embarrassed for not understanding, or because do not want to embarrass our conversation partner, or because we are trying to be efficient with our time.

Different conversation styles, mixed abilities and levels of English, and varied cross-cultural norms, all make international communication rather tricky and the likelihood of misunderstandings can be intensified. And these misunderstandings could potentially have very negative consequences, especially in the world of business.

When communicating internationally, try to:

● Clarify what you don't understand. You can say, *'I'm not sure if I understood what you mean,'* or, *'Could you explain what you mean by that?'*

● Clarify even when you think you've understood. If the speaker is making an important point (for example, terms of delivery, action points for a project), repeat back what you think you've understood. You can say, *'Let me check that I understood you correctly…'* or, *'Let me just repeat that back to you to make sure we both understood the same thing…'*

● Ask questions to clarify. Even if you understand the meaning of the words, you might not be sure what they are implying or how they feel about something. You could say, *'So I believe what you are saying is…'* or, *'Am I right to assume that you are not very keen on…?'*

❽ Paraphrase and summarise

Don't assume that your conversation partners are as confident at using the same clarification techniques that you do. Just because they are nodding, or smiling, or saying 'yes' to everything you are saying does not mean that they understand you.

When communicating internationally, try to:

● Make your point clearly. Be as explicit as you can without sounding patronising.

● Give reasons and/or examples to back up what you are saying.

● Repeat your point again using different words i.e. paraphrase.

- Be transparent about the fact that you are aware of the potential for misunderstandings in international communication, and that you are making an extra effort to be clear because it is an important point.

9 Accommodate and adapt to different ways of communicating

Different people have different communication styles and this might affect their speed, volume, pitch and intonation, their norms of turn-taking and interrupting, their use of indirect or direct ways of speaking, and their expectations of their conversation partners. Some of these differences will be addressed in Section III of this book, but be aware that sometimes when people have a different communication style to our own, it can be easy to get the wrong impression and assume they are rude, insincere, strange or even obnoxious.

When communicating internationally, try to:

- Refrain from judging someone based on how they speak.
- Become aware of your own style of communication.
- Spot the differences between their communication style and your own.
- Consider how you could adapt and accommodate.
- Be aware of their language ability. What do they understand and what do they have difficulty with? Can you make your message clearer to them by tailoring the language you use?

(In Chapter 2 you will be introduced to the ADAPT model, which can help you successfully manage international communication.)

10 Respect others

Communication is a two-way process. When communicating in English, those who are less fluent might find it more of an effort to interact, but those who are more proficient should not assume that they are in for an easy ride because of their language ability. The ability to treat people with respect is key to the relationships you forge and the reputation you gain.

When communicating internationally, try to:

- Remember that the level of someone's English is not a representation of their intelligence, their experience or their capabilities.
- Recognise their effort to speak in what is a foreign language to them.
- Avoid nit-picking and criticising their use of English.
- Remember that they might be using English but they are not necessarily familiar with your ways of communicating.

- Avoid judgement.
- Be respectful of the feelings of others.
- Show kindness and encourage when possible.

When writing or speaking about this issue, I have witnessed many occasions where native speakers of English have become offended or disgruntled by the suggestion that they could be the problem in a situation of international communication. Here, I would like to be clear that this is not about finger-pointing and putting the blame or the responsibility for successful communication on the native speaker. Neither is it about asking expert users of English to dumb down their language ability, or worse, use 'broken English', to communicate with less confident speakers.

International communication without the added obstacle of language issues is at best a multi-faceted area full of potential complications (some of which I will try to deal with in the rest of this book). Expert users of what is now the world's lingua franca could oil the wheels of communication by becoming more aware and reflective of their language use and playing their part in facilitating effective interactions.

I would like to end this section with a note for non-native speakers who are less confident with their use of English in international communication:

 Tips to remember

❶ Good communicators use their body language, their tone of voice and their facial expressions to get their message across. Don't be shy to speak just because you feel that your level of English is low.

❷ Don't feel like you have to change your accent to imitate a native speaker. Your accent is part of your identity and can be an interesting facet of your English. It is more important to work on pronouncing words in an intelligible way that will help you communicate internationally.

❸ Make your English your own. Consider:
- your motivations and your goals (*What kind of English do you want to learn? Why? What do you want to achieve?*)

- your communicative needs and purposes (*What do you need English for? Who will you speak to? What type of English would serve those needs?*)

- your learning situation (*How much time and effort can you spend on improving your English?*)

- how your English can express who you are (*Are you comfortable speaking English? Who do you want to be? Who is your role model?*).

4 There are many possible reasons for miscommunication. Your difficulty in understanding your conversation partner might not be due to your level of English. (I address some of these issues in the rest of this book.)

5 Bring elements of your own language and culture into your international conversations. Feel free to say, '*In my language, we have an idiom for this...*' or, '*I find this English expression funny because in my country...*'

6 Speak clearly. Listen actively. Do not be afraid to ask questions and to clarify. Paraphrase and summarise. Try to adapt to your conversation partners and show them respect. Many of the points in the list above apply to you too. After all, the success of communication is the joint responsibility of all the conversation partners involved.

Chapter 2: Intercultural awareness

What is culture?

One of the things I enjoy most in my career as a trainer is the opportunity to attend and speak at international teacher and trainer conferences. It is always heartening to see different people from different countries coming together to share their training expertise and experiences with others in the same profession. Although every conference speaker has their own style of presenting, it is a common belief among language and communication skills trainers that a good presenter often makes their point clearly, offers the audience chances for pair/group work and time to reflect, uses images cleverly in their slide deck, inspires their audience to put things in practice, and as a bonus, entertains them too. In the style of TED talks, the good presenter does not preach, lecture, overwhelm their audience with too much theory or bombard them with statistics, and certainly does not pack their slides with too many words or information. With every conference I attended, I found myself picking up presentation tips from the most successful presenters and modeling myself according to their presentation styles in order to become a better presenter.

After completing my Masters in Applied Linguistics in London, I was given the opportunity to present my thesis at a very different kind of conference: an academic conference held in Istanbul. I packed my presentation with amusing pictures, personal anecdotes and opportunities for the audience to work in pairs. By this point, I had become quite an experienced conference speaker in my own industry and was convinced that my presentation, along with my lively disposition, was going to strike a chord with my audience. As I attended other talks in the conference, I became mildly aware that the speakers were a lot more serious and focused very much on describing the parameters and the process of their research. Their slide decks were packed full of words and statistics with an average font size of 14, and there was absolutely no hint of witticisms, anecdotes or pair work in any of the talks. I ignorantly waved them off with the assumption that I had picked some rather boring presentations to go to and secretly celebrated my seemingly more dynamic presentation.

However, to my dismay, the audience who came to my talk was not as impressed with it as I myself had been. There were frowns all around the room and some puzzled faces as I put them in pairs to discuss the points I was making. Although some welcomed the lightness of my session, I suspect that they were dubious of my credibility as a researcher, saw me as a frivolous presenter, and did not take my results very seriously. I had made the fundamental error of assuming that what was considered a good presentation in the practitioners' world would automatically be so in the academic world.

The practitioners' world and the academics' one had differing practices and operated under separate rules when it came to conference presentations. Naturally, the consequent evaluation of the presenters also varied depending on the corresponding expectations. While I found the academic presentations boring and irrelevant to my daily practice, the academic audience found my presentations flippant and lacking in rigour. Our two industries had different cultural expectations of what comprised of a good presentation; what I had experienced was a version of culture clash.

When intercultural communication is discussed, we often assume that we are talking about national cultures: the Spanish are like this and the Chinese are like that, missing the fact that culture is a construct that could be associated with a group of people who are not necessarily bound by a common nationality. In the story above, my intercultural experience was a result of different cultural practices in two different industries.

Defining culture

There are many definitions of *culture*, but my favourite one is by Professor Helen Spencer-Oatey[10] who describes culture as, '*a fuzzy set of basic assumptions and values, orientations to life, beliefs, policies, procedures and behavioural conventions that are shared by a group of people, and that influence (but do not determine) each member's behaviour and his/her interpretations of the "meaning" of other people's behaviour*'.

It is key to remember that no two people sharing the same nationality or profession share the exact same characteristics. However, our belonging to a social group can certainly serve as a filter, affecting how we act and how we see the world, not unlike a pair of tailor-made filtered lenses that interpret what we perceive, placing selective focus on some aspects more than others.

---

10 Spencer-Oatey H (2008) Introduction. In: H Spencer Oatey (ed.) *Culturally Speaking: Culture, Communication and Politeness Theory* (2nd edn) pp1–8. London: Continuum.

Aside from national culture and industry culture, there are also many other cultural filters that could influence our belief systems, our attitudes, our rituals and our behaviours. The company we work for, the department we belong to, the region we come from, our age, gender, ethnic group, religion, class, political affiliation, profession, interests and hobbies can all shape what we do and how we experience the world around us.

Yet, when discussing intercultural communication, there seems be an immediate presumption of national stereotypes. Whenever I deliver workshops with titles like 'Presenting across cultures', 'Cross-cultural negotiations' or 'Intercultural team management', participants often start off with the assumption that I am about to present them with a list of dos and don'ts categorised according to country. They want an easy-to-follow instruction manual that says, *'If you are negotiating with the Russians, do these five things and you won't go wrong'.*

Of course, if simplified generalisations are what they are looking for, a quick online search would bring up lots of tables and visually arresting infographics that offer an insight into the rituals and practices of certain national cultures, however accurate: in China, always give and receive business cards with both hands; in France you should always dress well; in Venezuela, don't show up on time, etc. I suppose it is human nature to want clear categories and a quick-and-easy recipe that tells us exactly what to do and the results we can expect. Unfortunately, human beings are a lot more complicated, and convenient expedients could end up being the source of inaccurate and unhelpful stereotypes and misrepresentations.

Being in the middle of a culture clash

National culture can undoubtedly be the cause of culture clashes too, but it is important that we delve a bit deeper to understand the reasons behind the clash and not stop at simply judging what seems foreign to us. Before I began my career as a communication skills trainer, I spent a couple of months based in a factory in Japan working for a large American IT company. The American company had been hired by the Japanese factory to rebuild their networks but was having problems communicating with the people there. Assuming that the breakdown in communication was due to language issues, they hired me as an interpreter, but within the first few days of my stay it was clear to me that the problems they were having were not language-related. Many of the Japanese involved in the project spoke fluent English and were just as frustrated that they were not able to get through to the Americans. (Note that when I refer to *the Americans* and *the Japanese* in this story, I am strictly referring to the Americans and the Japanese who were working on this project and not to every citizen of those two nations.)

As both sides started to confide in me, these were some of the things I realised were happening:

- For the Americans, meetings in this Japanese factory were too long. Whether it was a meeting to introduce a new member to the team, a meeting to work out a plan, or a meeting to make a decision, the Americans felt that their time was being wasted in the meeting rooms talking and not acting. To them, this was disrespectful of the precious time they had in Japan to get their job done.

- For the Japanese, the Americans seemed impatient and brash. The Japanese felt the Americans were prone to making rash decisions before any careful planning or thinking, and that their actions would end up costing their company millions. This was disrespectful of every individual on that team who had invested time and effort into the project.

- For the Americans, the Japanese were not upfront about what their intentions were and not honest about how they felt. Whenever a proposal was made, the Japanese would never voice a clear yes or no. They might seem agreeable in a meeting, but would oppose the suggestion in a later email. The Americans saw this as deceitful behaviour that did not contribute to team morale.

- For the Japanese, the Americans were rude and selfish. They would boldly state their disagreement even at the cost of making the Japanese look bad in front of the rest of the team and hurting their feelings. The Japanese were shocked that the Americans seemed to care only about their own personal point of view and not consider the points of view of the team, and saw this as egotistical behaviour that damaged team morale.

Both parties were clearly operating under different norms and had different expectations of each other's behaviour. However, the Americans and the Japanese on my team did what most people facing an intercultural clash would do: they made a judgment of the other's behaviour based on their own values, norms and beliefs, and they did not go on to then consider the different set of values and norms that underlie the other party's behaviour.

The Cultural Iceberg

An analogy often used to describe the phenomenon of an intercultural clash is the 'Cultural Iceberg'[11] model.

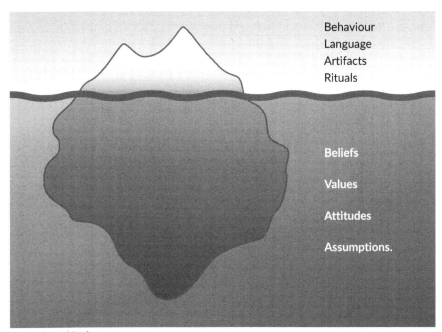

Behaviour
Language
Artifacts
Rituals

Beliefs

Values

Attitudes

Assumptions.

The cultural iceberg

The top 20% of the iceberg represents what is visible of a culture or social group. This comprises the behaviour (an orientation towards careful planning versus an orientation towards quick action, a direct versus an indirect style of communication, etc.), the artefacts (the food, the music and art, the festivals, the language, etc.) and the rituals (the customs, the practices, the way things are normally done, etc.) of the group. The top of the iceberg is what we can see, hear or touch and what is immediately observable by others from outside the group.

The majority of the iceberg is however not as easily observable to others. This includes the attitudes, the beliefs, the values and the motivations, some of which might be unconscious even to those in the in-group. Although invisible

---

11 Originally developed by Edward T Hall in Hall ET (1976). *Beyond culture*. Garden City, N.Y: Anchor Press.

to many, these parts below the waterline can provide an explanation and a deeper understanding towards behaviour, artefacts and rituals that might initially seem foreign and even *wrong* to those from a different *iceberg*.

Our tendency to focus solely on the differences in the behaviour of *the other* and make quick judgments based on our own cultural lenses can be detrimental to our relationships and unproductive for our work. Eventually, this can result in a breakdown in communication, like in the case of the Americans and Japanese in the team. An attempt to dig deeper (into the iceberg) and understand each other's underlying beliefs and values about how a team should work together would have revealed the following:

> The Americans believed that meetings should be efficient, and being productive meant acting on something and not just talking about it (see Chapter 4). They believed that by actually doing it, they would then be able to tailor the subsequent steps based on what worked and what didn't work. The Americans on the project also believed in each member having the right to speak their mind and that being direct is equivalent to being genuine and honest (see Chapter 5).
>
> Conversely, the Japanese at this factory were keen planners and believed that it was important to think each step through carefully, planning right through until the end before taking action (see Chapter 4). They believed in the importance of team agreement (see Chapter 9) and felt that there isn't always a need to be brusque and direct about one's opinions. They considered the ability to read between the lines as the mark of an educated and refined person (see Chapter 5).
>
> It is important to recognise that not all Americans and Japanese share the above beliefs and would behave in the same manner as the team in Japan. Even the same people when placed in a different context with different people might behave in a very different way. The skill of intercultural communication is therefore not about making sweeping generalisations of one culture and imposing presuppositions about their actions to neatly explain away puzzling behaviour.

Culture is not limited to nationality, nor is it static and unchanging. There are a variety of cultural filters (their age, their social group, their industry, their nationality, etc.) influencing the individual, and the beliefs and attitudes of these different cultures can combine in a variety of ways, depending on the situation and the people involved in the interaction. When two or more people communicate, they might have certain expectations of how the conversation might unfold based on their past experiences. However, interactions are dynamic and not always predictable, and the individuals might find themselves adapting to the new rules of communication and improvising as the conversation progresses.

The ability to adapt and accommodate is one of the key skills to being an effective international communicator; but before we are able to adapt, we must first be able to see the issues we are facing and have an awareness of what is causing the problem, and this isn't always as easy as it seems. A joke retold by many cultural trainers exemplifies this perfectly: two fish meet each other as they are swimming along. One fish asks the other, 'How's the water today?' to which the other fish replies, 'What is water?'.

Like the fish, we are not always aware of our norms, our routines, our behaviour and our expectations, and how they differ to others. Taking the fish out of water and placing them in a different liquid will no doubt be a quick way of making the fish aware of what it had been taking for granted. Similarly, many colleagues and friends have reported feeling a stronger belonging to their cultural groups when taken out of their comfort zones. The ability to develop a self-awareness of our inherent beliefs and attitudes and how they can affect our behaviour and expectations of others is the first step towards improving our intercultural competence, and in order to do so, we sometimes need to be confronted with a different set of beliefs, attitudes and resulting behaviour to clearly see the water we are swimming in.

Cultural frameworks and dimensions

There are elements of culture that are variable and fluid and can change over time, but certain values may remain constant across different contexts and have powerful effects on the behaviour of people from a particular cultural group. Over the years, researchers and writers from a variety of fields ranging from anthropology and psychology to business studies and linguistics have suggested different key dimensions of culture that could help us understand our differences by breaking down and categorising the different orientations in a person's beliefs and values.

Anthropologist Edward T Hall[12], who started writing about inter-cultural communication in the 1950s, psychologist Geert Hofstede[13], who collected a worldwide survey of IBM employees in the 1960s and 70s, and management consultant Fons Trompenaars[14], who became well-known in the business sector in the 1990s for his model of national culture differences, are examples of influential intercultural authors of varied backgrounds whose works have provided possible frameworks for thinking about cultural diversity. Below is a brief overview of a selection of cultural dimensions that can be most apparent when communicating internationally, especially in business. (Note, they will be re-visited and explored in more depth together with some key interpersonal skills in the rest of the book.)

While there is a general tendency across these different frameworks to mean *national culture* when *culture* is being discussed, we should look beyond national culture and use the following cultural dimensions as a tool for helping us better appreciate the differences between how we see the world. Most of these cultural dimensions are presented as a scale, with the extremes at the two opposing ends. This suggests that some cultural groups might belong on the far end of a scale whilst others might remain near the middle.

It is also vital that we remember that orientations on these dimensions are meant to be prototypes of a cultural group: some members of the group will display more of its features and be more representative of certain orientations than others, seeing that no group of people are uniform in their behaviour or their values and beliefs. Also, we must not forget that cultural groups and societies can change over time, and sometimes this can happen quite rapidly with modern influences like globalisation and the internet.

---

12 Hall ET (1976) *Beyond Culture*. Garden City, N.Y: Anchor Press.

13 Hofstede GH (2001) *Culture's Consequences: Comparing values, behaviors, institutions, and organizations across nations.* Thousand Oaks, Calif: Sage Publications.

14 Trompenaars A (1994) *Riding the Waves of Culture: Understanding diversity in global business.* Burr Ridge, Ill: Irwin Professional Pub.

As you read the descriptions of each of the cultural dimensions below, consider the following questions:

- What do you think people from one end of the scale might say of people from the other end of the scale? What words might they use to describe each other?
- Have you encountered people who have such different attitudes? Did it cause any problems? How did you deal with it?

Low-context communication ➤ High-context communication

First suggested by Hall, this is a dimension used to describe how some people communicate. People used to low-context communication tend to use explicit and overt messages and responses when getting meaning across. You say what you mean and simplicity and clarity is seen as key to good communication. People used to high-context communication, however, tend to use implicit messages and metaphors. They rely heavily on contextual cues, non-verbal communication, and pre-existing knowledge and experience to convey meaning. In other words, you are expected to read between the lines in order to understand what is said.

Individualism ➤ Collectivism

A cultural dimension that was first written about by Hall, and subsequently by Trompenaars, who then re-framed it with the terms *Individualism versus Communitarianism*, this is a framework for how we see our relationship to others and to our communities and our society. People from individualistic societies tend to focus on their own needs, wants and preferences and are responsible for their own welfare. People from collectivist societies tend to see themselves as part of a larger unit, e.g. the family, the team, the department and/or the community. Loyalty and support within the unit is expected and priority is given to the needs and goals of the group.

High power distance ➤ Low power distance

Describing differences in the way we relate to authority figures such as our parents, our teachers and our managers, the power distance dimension was first developed by Geert Hofstede but has since been expanded on by writers like Erin Meyer[15] in her book *The Culture Map*, where she uses the *Egalitarian versus Hierarchical* scale to frame the way we see our leaders and our bosses. Cultural groups with high power distance tend to be hierarchical and tend to expect and accept the inequality in the distribution of power. Everyone

15 Erin Meyer (2014) *The Culture Map*. United States of America: Public Affairs.

has a role to play and there is no need for justification of their place in the hierarchical order of things. Low power distance groups, on the other hand, strive for equal distribution of power. Members of high status like managers are expected to consider their employees as equals and involve them equally in decision-making processes.

High uncertainty avoidance ⟨▬▬▬▬▬⟩ Low uncertainty avoidance

Another cultural dimension theorised by Geert Hofstede, this relates to how we deal with ambiguity and the unfamiliar. People tending towards high uncertainty avoidance would prefer structures, rules and conventions. They dislike circumstances that are unpredictable, uncertain or unknown and might feel uncomfortable with unconventional ways of thinking and acting. People with low uncertainty avoidance are inclined to be open to change and innovation and don't feel a need to control the future. They may also tend to be more at ease when communicating with people who are different from themselves.

Linear time ⟨▬▬▬▬▬▬▬⟩ Flexible time

Hall first wrote about a similar scale that he named *Monochronic Time (M-Time) versus Polychronic Time (P-Time)*, and later, Trompenaars proposed a related cultural dimension that he called *Sequential Time versus Synchronous Time*. Here, I have chosen the terms put forward by Erin Meyer[16] as they explain the concept clearly and succinctly. People of a linear time culture tend to do one thing at a time and prefer to plan and schedule activities, and see time in a linear fashion. Time is seen as a limited resource and needs to be used efficiently. On the contrary, people with an attitude of flexible time tend to multi-task and do several things at once. While it is important to complete tasks, there is less emphasis on deadlines and when things get done.

Long-term orientation ⟨▬▬▬▬▬⟩ Short-term orientation

In 1991, Hofstede wrote about the way a cultural group's values might be oriented towards future rewards, or conversely be related to the past and present[17]. People with long-term orientations tend to focus on the future, prioritising working hard to prepare for the future. Virtues like persistence and thrift are valued, and the ability to solve problems and adapt to different circumstances are a necessity. In contrast, people with short-term orientations tend to focus on the past and the present, preferring to stick to how things

---

16 Ibid.

17 Geert Hofstede (2001) *Culture's Consequences*, 2nd ed.:p 359. Thousand Oaks CA: Sage Publications.

have always been done, and viewing change with suspicion. Steadfastness is important, truth is absolute, and you should remain faithful to your fixed norms and traditions.

Task orientation vs Relationship orientation

In addition to the six that I've chosen to briefly summarise, there are also cultural dimensions that deal with how we distinguish work and relationships. In Trompenaars's[18] dimension of *Specific versus Diffuse*, he explored the way some might keep work and relationships separate while others see good relationships and good business going hand in hand. Meyer[19] looked at the different ways we build trust and concluded that some people tend to have a task-based approach while others have a relationship-based approach. However, instead of looking at this dimension in the form of a scale where the two ends oppose each other, we could consider approaching this from the perspective of a symbiosis.

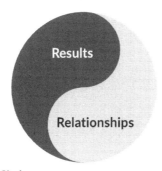

The Relationship-Results Circle

While some people might tend to focus more on tasks and results, others might find it more important to focus on relationships. The two, however, are interdependent on each other. They might be seemingly opposite traits in the circle, but they both work in harmony to form a balanced whole. In many cases you would not be able to get the results you want if you do not cultivate the relationship with your partner, or you might risk the relationship if you do not achieve the expected results. A breakdown in one could, after all, lead to a breakdown in the other.

18 Trompenaars A (1994) *Riding the Waves of Culture: Understanding diversity in global business.* Burr Ridge, Ill: Irwin Professional Pub.

19 Erin Meyer (2014) *The Culture Map.* United States of America: Public Affairs

Like many aspects of culture, these two are not fixed and unchanging. They are fluid and can ebb and flow at any given moment. So how can we then choose to deal with this ebb and flow? The balance we strike between how much focus we place on results and how much we nurture our relationships can be a tricky one as it might depend entirely on the circumstances you are in and the people you are dealing with. Too much focus on one might come at the cost of the other. The following Critical Incident is an example of how balancing the two can sometimes be a juggling act and a difference in focus between two people can cause problems.

 Look at the critical incident below. What do you think of Ferris's efforts to adapt? What had he failed to consider?

Ferris was put in an international team and had to work closely with Max. In a face-to-face meeting with Ferris, Max spent a lot of time getting to know him, asking questions about his family and his hobbies, suggesting they go out for dinner and drinks. Ferris, however, was more keen to dive in and talk about the project. He had flown in from another continent and didn't want to waste any time on small talk. He understood the importance of relationship building but found it more important to get things done first. As a result of their difference in focus, Max and Ferris's relationship was compromised and the project suffered serious delays.

Upon returning to his country, Ferris reflected on the experience and realised that, for Max, getting to know his partner was key to building trust and setting the foundation for a good working relationship. He recognised that he could perhaps have been more sensitive to Max's need for more relationship building whilst not losing sight of their work targets. A year later, Ferris flew over to meet Max to finalise the completion of the project. This time, Ferris worked hard to ask questions about Max's family, find out about Max's hobbies and suggested going out for lunch together. To his surprise, Max was not as keen on talking about his personal life and was instead focused on getting the project completed and signed off.

What Ferris had not taken into account was the fact that their circumstances had changed. His second trip was made to wrap up the project. With strict deadlines in place, Max was feeling stressed and under pressure to complete the remaining tasks and was more focused on the results that needed to be achieved. Although Ferris did well in making the attempt to reflect and then adapt to what he thought Max's preferences were, he was not able to react according to the ebb and flow of the circumstances when confronted with the fact that the very same person (Max) could be relationship-oriented in one instance, and results-oriented in another.

The cultural dimensions above could provide us with some ways of looking at culture but we should always remember that culture is a construct that is multifaceted, changeable and dynamic. When two people come together in an interaction, they bring with them a range of behaviours, expectations, values, beliefs and attitudes that are influenced by their different cultural associations (e.g. gender, age, nationality, occupation, social groups). Yet these behaviours, expectations, values, etc. are by no means static or fixed; they change to adapt to the people and situations we are in.

There are multiple intercultural researchers and models that offer us different frameworks of culture, but it isn't necessary or possible to know every single one of them. What is key is the ability to develop a set of behaviours that can help you face any kind of diversity you come into contact with when communicating interculturally.

Intercultural competence

Intercultural Interaction Competence is a term often used by academics to describe one's proficiency at dealing with intercultural interactions. Spencer-Oatey and Franklin[20] suggest that this refers to one's ability to communicate verbally and non-verbally, behave effectively and appropriately with people from other cultural groups, and also the ability to handle the psychological demands and dynamic outcomes that result from these interactions.

---

20 Spencer-Oatey H & Franklin P (2009) *Intercultural Interaction: A multidisciplinary approach to intercultural communication.* London: Palgrave Macmillan

So, how can we become more interculturally competent? What skills or attitudes do we need to develop to be able to behave appropriately or handle the psychological demands of such interactions? Scholars and researchers of multiple disciplines have put forward their own lists of components that make up intercultural competence. Over my years of interacting with clients from different cultural backgrounds and delivering intercultural communication skills training, I have also found certain skills extremely pertinent to the development of an effective international communicator.

Top ten skills for the intercultural communicator to cultivate

❶ Self-awareness and the ability to reflect

The journey to becoming a more effective intercultural communicator has to begin with self-awareness. Defined by Psychologist Daniel Goleman[21] as 'knowing one's internal states, preferences, resources and intuitions', self-awareness is about understanding our own behaviours, feelings and thoughts, and the underlying motivations, causes and reasons behind them. This includes knowing your own tendencies, prejudices and biases, and strengths and weaknesses.

A better understanding of ourselves can go a long way in helping us comprehend our reactions and responses to intercultural situations. Without self-awareness, we could go on pointing the finger at others and blaming them for their ways without realising that we ourselves could very well be the cause of the problem. And in order to become more self-aware, we need to be able to reflect on our experiences and our mistakes and learn from them.

❷ Curiosity: finding out about 'the other'

Aside from knowing about ourselves, we also need to know more about the people we are interacting with. We need to be able to go beyond the tip of the iceberg (**—>** see The Cultural Iceberg on page 31) and understand the underlying reasons for their behaviour and practices. This process starts with having an inherent curiosity about 'the other' and wanting to get to know them better.

The information gathering could take place before, during or after the interactions, and could include reading articles and books like this one, or having open conversations with your conversation partners, or even people

---

21 Goleman D (1995) *Emotional Intelligence*. USA: Bantam Books.

from the same cultural group, about their norms, their processes, their expectations and their values, attitudes and beliefs. This process might take time and effort but could help you avoid jumping to the wrong conclusions or making unhelpful judgements of 'the other'.

❸ Mindfulness and perceptiveness

When communicating interculturally, we need to be able to be aware of our own and the other's behaviour, the ways we are communicating (What are we really saying? What does that intonation mean?), the way we are coming across to others, and the possibilities for miscommunication and misunderstanding. In a way, mindfulness combines the first two skills on this list, and puts them into practice in an on-going interaction. Perceptiveness refers to an ability to attune ourselves to what is happening, and a sensitivity to the circumstances, the context and our conversation partners.

❹ Open-mindedness and non-judgementalness

It might be difficult to see things in a different way when we have been so used to our own view of the world for our entire life. But a willingness to try, and to accept that there are others who may see the world differently requires a level of open-mindedness. Such an attitude of openness can lead us to put aside our prejudices and biases, suspend the judgments of 'the other', and embrace ideas, practices and approaches which are new and unfamiliar. (→See 'Dealing with intercultural communication' on page 43 for more detail on how to put this into practice.)

❺ Patience and tolerance for ambiguity

Life isn't always black and white and we often encounter different shades of grey that might not be as defined as we would like them to be. There may not be a right or wrong way of doing things but sometimes it is tempting to think that our way is the better one. Other than being patient and respectful of different approaches and attitudes, we could also benefit from the ability to feel comfortable in ambiguous situations where things seem complicated, uncertain and unpredictable.

When dropped into unfamiliar situations where the behaviour of the other seems to be governed by an unknown framework and where we are unsure of how to interpret their signals and cues, we need avoid reacting to them as if they are a threat. Instead, we could find ways of becoming more tolerant of diversity and of the unknown.

⑥ Emotional strength

The anxiety of dealing with the unfamiliar, the embarrassment of being misunderstood, and the stress of coping with the unexpected can all be overwhelming, and for some of us there is the temptation to walk away from it all and yell, '*It's not me, it's them*'. Emotional strength refers to the resilience we have within us to take problems in our stride, deal with them, move ahead with our objectives in mind, learn from our mistakes, and remain calm and optimistic throughout.

⑦ Interpersonal skills

While an intercultural communicator might not need to be extremely gregarious or outgoing, it would be helpful to have the social skills needed to build relationships and foster trust. This involves building rapport, creating bonds that go towards eliminating the sense of 'us' and 'them', empathising with others, and maintaining relationships. (These will be covered in detail in later chapters.)

⑧ Core communication skills

It would be hard to be an effective intercultural communicator without some core communication skills. This includes the ability to create understanding and be clear and transparent, the awareness of the different communication conventions involved, and the sensitivity to detect misunderstandings and repair them when necessary. (For more information ➔see Chapter 1, page 18, and Chapter 5.)

⑨ Flexibility and adaptability

How easy is it for you to accommodate other points of view? How quickly can you adapt your behaviour or your communication style to suit the different situations you are in? Combined with the skills above, are you able to re-think and question the stereotypes you might have? The flexibility and adaptability to modify our assumptions and adjust our behaviour is often the proof that we are able to put what we know about intercultural interactions into practice. (The final part of this chapter on intercultural awareness looks at some ways that can help you achieve this.)

⑩ Sense of identity and objectives

A common question I often get in my intercultural seminars is, '*Why should the responsibility to adapt and change lie with me? Why can't the other party change to suit my ways?*' My reply often resembles a version of the following: you can't control what others might do, but you are in control of your own thoughts and behaviour. As we say in English, charity starts at home. If we make an attempt to adapt, it will signal a willingness to work together and this might inspire and motivate others to do the same. However, sometimes my clients would reply, *'But that would mean changing who I am to suit others. Isn't that dishonest?'*

My response might seem contradictory to Point 9 above but it isn't: *Be yourself!* Be true to your values and your beliefs and remember who you are. But also know that there are different versions of yourself. There is the *you* who is a manager of a team, the *you* who is a friend to others, the *you* who is the child to your parent, the *you* who is a parent to your child, etc. Each facet of yourself engages in interactions differently depending on the situation you find yourself in. In an intercultural interaction, you need to be ready to adapt this version of *you* to facilitate communication and achieve the objectives of the interaction. Sometimes, we can do this by finding similarities between our goals or our values and beliefs and those of *the other*, or we could value our differences as assets that would add value to our interactions. In this new relationship, we can come together to create a culture that works for us.

Dealing with intercultural communication

When confronted with behaviours that are different to expectations, many of us might be tempted to judge that behaviour according to our own norms, beliefs and assumptions.

 Consider the critical incident below. How do you think Alice can overcome her feelings of discomfort?

When Alice started working in the UK, she enjoyed having lunch with her new colleagues in the break room, but she was struck by how different their washing-up routine was from her own. They would fill a sink up with water and some washing-up liquid, then they would put all the dirty dishes and cutlery into the sink. One person would volunteer to wash the dishes and put them onto the drying rack. This made Alice very uncomfortable because she was used to rinsing each dish under running water after scrubbing them individually with a sponge. The idea of having all the dishes sitting in a pool of dirty water and the sight of soap suds still on the dishes on the rack disgusted Alice and she concluded that her colleagues were unhygienic, lazy and dirty.

💬 When faced with strange and unfamiliar behaviour, like in the case of Alice and the dishes, the DIE[1] model is one that can be used to help raise awareness of our cultural assumptions and encourage us to gather other possible interpretations and reasons for the behaviour in question. Commonly used in intercultural training, the DIE model, standing for *Describe, Interpret, Evaluate*, can encourage us to withhold our immediate responses and to take time to consider possible reasons for what we see.

In a situation of a culture clash, many of us might react in the same way Alice did. After witnessing her colleagues' method of washing up, she immediately jumped to a conclusion and made a quick judgment, presenting her feelings about her colleagues as factual information about them. She had essentially dived from the *Describe* stage of the DIE model straight into the *Evaluate* stage, skipping the *Interpret* stage completely.

Alice's cultural experience may seem unimportant or even trivial to some of us, but it was one of things that really bothered her and prevented her from building a stronger bond with her colleagues. After some intercultural skills training, Alice was able to take a step back and consider the situation and write down the following:

Describe
(What did you observe?)

My colleagues washing up by putting all the dishes in a sink full of soapy water, wiping them and putting them on a drying rack.

Interpret
(What do you think might be the reasons for this behaviour?)

1. My colleagues are using the most time-efficient way to wash everyone's dishes all at once.

2. My colleagues are trying to save water.

3. My colleagues come from households where there were two sinks, one for soapy water and one for rinsing water, but they had to improvise because there was only one sink at work.

4. My colleagues saw their predecessors doing it that way and so was just doing what was usually done in this office.

Evaluate
(How do you feel about this?)

*Note the numbers below correspond to the numbers on the left.

1. It's nice of them to think of washing everyone's dishes and not just their own. Not only this, but I think it's important to save time because we all need to get back to work.

2. I like the idea of looking after our environment and not wasting water.

3. I feel uncomfortable taking dishes from a pool of dirty water and putting them straight on the rack. I think they need to improvise in a different way.

4. It's important to continue traditions but I don't think people should do things just because that's the way it's always been done. I feel they should be embarrassed that they're doing something so unhygienic.

---

1 This model was first used in intercultural training by Janet M Bennett and Milton Bennett for workshops at the University of Minnesota. See also Bennett JM, Bennett MJ & Stillings K (1977) *Intercultural Communication Workshop Facilitator's Annual*. Portland, OR: Portland State University.

Some of Alice's evaluations were positive and some were negative, and they were based on her feelings and therefore neither right nor wrong. However, the process of doing this exercise forced Alice to suspend any judgments and try as far as possible to describe the situation and the behaviour as objectively as she could. She then had to consider the possible reasons and underlying causes for that behaviour. In doing so, she had to put herself in their shoes and empathise. She also had to try to gather information and this might have involved her talking to her colleagues openly about the reasons for their behaviour. In evaluating their behaviour, she became aware of her own norms, values and beliefs and consequently how judgmental she had previously been. Now, look back at the top ten skills on page 40 again. Which of those skills do you think Alice might have cultivated from using the DIE model?

Using models for guidance

The DIE model can be excellent for encouraging reflection and raising awareness, and for developing curiosity, patience, perceptiveness and openness, but sometimes it's hard to know how we can go from that to actually adapting our behaviour. So, I have developed the ADAPT model to help us do just that.

The ADAPT Model

Awareness	Be aware of what I am feeling. What was I expecting? What might they be expecting? What might they be thinking of me?
Don't judge	Refrain from jumping to conclusions. What are my prejudices? What stereotypes might I have that might affect my understanding?
Analyse	Explore the underlying reasons behind their behaviour. Why do they do this? What can I do to find out more? How can I deepen my understanding?
Persuade yourself	Aim to align yourself more with this behaviour. Are there similarities to what I do in other contexts or my attitudes to other things? Do I relate to some of the reasons for their behaviour?
Try	Consider changing the way you think about something or even the way you behave. How can you adapt in such a way that allows you to remain true to yourself? Try being a bit flexible and you will find that sometimes a small change is all it takes.

Applying the ADAPT model, Alice did the following:

Applying the ADAPT model

Awareness

I am used to washing up a certain way and was expecting my colleagues to do it my way. If they see my way of washing up, they might think I am overly particular about cleanliness or that I am wasteful with water.

Don't judge

I am making the assumption that putting all the dishes in the soapy water was dirty and unhygienic. There's actually no evidence for that. I'm also assuming they are doing it because they are lazy but I don't necessarily know that.

Analyse

They might be doing it to save water, or to save time. Maybe they are trying to think of our office as a community and are doing it to help everyone else. Or maybe they are just doing it because that's how it's always been done? Maybe I should speak to someone I'm close to in the office and find out why this is the way they do it.

Persuade yourself

I like the idea of saving water and saving time. It is important to look after our environment as well as being efficient with our lunch break. After all, we all have a lot of work to get back to. I also like the idea that this method of washing up allows us to do a large load at one time, which means we can help our colleagues save time too. I think this is important to me because it will help me understand and get along with my colleagues better.

Try

Maybe I can volunteer tomorrow to wash up the dishes after we have all had our lunch, but instead of just putting the dishes straight from the water onto the rack, I'm going to rinse them quickly in batches so that I don't waste too much water.

In applying the ADAPT model, Alice was able to reconcile the differences that she initially found uncomfortable and was able to find her own way of adapting to a different way of thinking and doing things. Now go back to the list of top ten skills on page 40 again and see if you can identify the skills that Alice managed to put into practice.

In the rest of this book I will be exploring eight different interpersonal communication skills and also looking at the possible intercultural differences that might surface. Try applying the ADAPT model to some of the critical incidents presented and consider what and how you might adapt in those situations.

Chapter 3: Building relationships

The importance of relationships

I grew up in Singapore — a society that is in love with food. Eating out is practically considered a national sport and parents show their love for their children by taking them to the best restaurants. When I was a child, my grandmother's favourite way of connecting with me was to ask, '*Where do you want to go for lunch?*' Social conversations often revolve around where one can find the best *rendang/chicken rice/laksa*. Food and relationships are closely associated and it is commonplace for business people to build relationships over a meal. I remember a famous Singaporean businessman once said something to the tune of, '*When I started to get fat, my business started to grow*'. After all, growing a business often required a lot of wining and dining of clients and associates.

When I landed my first full-time job as a trainer in London, I quickly realised that the fastest way of forming strong relationships with my colleagues was to head to a bar with them every evening where I got to know them, and all the ins and outs of the company, over a drink or two. Although a different 'medium' was the norm in my new environment, there was also an understanding that good relationships are the foundation of business success. Ultimately, human beings are social creatures and when we develop good working relationships we find ourselves feeing more positive, enjoying our work more, understanding and relating to each other better, communicating more effectively and working together more successfully.

First impressions

For many people, the first step can be the most intimidating. Speaking to someone we don't yet have a relationship with can feel awkward and uncomfortable. Yet first impressions can be very important. Some say that it takes only seven seconds to make a first impression, and those first impressions often stick. In order to tackle this potentially nerve-racking first meeting, consider applying the stages of my ICE-BREAK mnemonic:

* Introduce yourself
* Comment on a mutual area of commonality
* Encourage participation

* Balance between questions and comments
* Reveal something about yourself
* Express curiosity and interest
* Ask open-ended questions
* Keep your answers short and simple

ICE-BREAK - Getting to know someone

Ice-breaking in practice

Let us consider the eight stages of ICE-BREAK in further detail.

1   Introduce yourself

The first step when meeting someone new is to introduce ourselves and in some cases exchange business cards. (NB: you might want to do some online research into the cultures that expect you to give and receive business cards with both hands[22].) If your new conversation partner hands you a business card without explicitly saying, 'Hello, I'm Michelle,' it might be up to you to decide how to address her.

---

22 For example: http://uk.businessinsider.com/a-guide-to-business-etiquette-around-the-world-2015-5

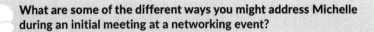

What are some of the different ways you might address Michelle during an initial meeting at a networking event?

RAMSDEN & GRIFFIN LTD

Dr. Michelle Kathleen Kowalski

When we meet someone for the first time, we have certain expectations of how they might address us – and these expectations might be based on a variety of factors, from the way we are usually addressed in our company and the norms in our country to our preferred management styles and our personal preferences. You might find that Michelle prefers to use her middle name 'Kathleen', or that she is used to people she doesn't know well calling her 'Dr Kowalski', or that she prefers the informality of 'Dr Michelle'. Perhaps it is common in her country for those of lower status to address her as 'Mdm Director', or maybe she prefers not to focus on status differences and would rather be called 'Michelle' by everybody. So if Michelle Kathleen Kowalski was addressed in a way that she wasn't expecting, she might find it amusing and brush it off, she might wince or cringe and put it down to cultural differences, or she might assume that her conversation partner was being disrespectful.

In one of my intercultural training sessions, my participants got into a heated debate about the use of the title Dr to address someone with a doctorate. One of my participants was adamant that one should only actively use the title Dr if they were medical doctors, and that people with doctorates who wanted to be addressed as Dr were full of themselves. He believed the use of such a title on a business card was a sign of arrogance, and insisted that a business card like Michelle's would leave a very bad impression on him. A couple of participants nodded in agreement, but the other participants found this train of thought puzzling. They argued that people who have worked hard to earn their doctorate degree deserved to reap the benefits that come with it, and that it would be rude not to address someone with a doctorate with their appropriate title, especially when meeting them for the first time. It was interesting how strongly each participant felt about their standpoint, and how surprising they found the opposing points of view.

To avoid a potential faux pas, ensure that you listen carefully to how your conversation partner introduces themselves and how they address you. Be mindful of their reactions when you address them and do not be afraid to ask them how they would like to be addressed if necessary. Eliminate any doubt by offering information about how you'd like to be addressed right from the start by saying something like, 'Hi, I'm Michelle Kowalski but most people just call me Kathleen'. And if you encounter someone who addresses you in a way you find uncomfortable, be aware that it is often because they are operating based on their own norms and expectations, and not because they are intentionally disrespecting you.

2   Comment on a mutual area of commonality

After the initial introductions, some people make use of the age-old ritual of small talk to generate some positive feelings and help put everyone at ease. The Merriam-Webster dictionary defines small talk as light and casual conversation[23] and Wikipedia suggests that small talk is conversation for its own sake[24]. The aim of small talk is to establish rapport with our conversation partner: to show that we have something in common and we are on the same wavelength. However, the way we go about doing so might differ from group to group.

---

23 https://www.merriam-webster.com/dictionary/small%20talk
24 https://en.wikipedia.org/wiki/Small_talk

Read Joanna's account below and consider what might have gone wrong in her first meeting with Kwang?

I was at a networking event and I saw Kwang standing there looking lonely so I thought I'd go and talk to him. I said hello and we introduced ourselves. Suddenly, he asked me how old I was. I didn't know how to react so I laughed. Then Kwang said he didn't understand why I was laughing because he didn't make a joke. So I said sorry and excused myself.

That first encounter unfortunately did not seem leave a good impression on Joanna or Kwang, and both were left feeling awkward and uncomfortable. While Kwang did not share Joanna's usage of laughter to diffuse awkwardness (see → 'Use of humour' on page 62), there was also clearly a different understanding of what topics were appropriate for small talk.

To Joanna, age was a private matter and a sensitive one to some, and in her culture it was common knowledge that one does not openly ask a woman her age, especially during a first meeting. To Kwang, knowledge of his conversation partner's age was crucial in helping him understand where he stands in comparison. Coming from a hierarchical culture where age is an important factor in determining where one stands in the social hierarchy of things, Kwang felt that he needed to know Joanna's age so that he could address her appropriately and speak to her with the right amount of deference.

Which of these topics of conversation do you consider acceptable when making small talk? Which of these topics would make you uncomfortable in a conversation? Why?

your parents' health

the price of your car

politics

football

weather

your age

travel plans

your children's education

religion

the latest technological devices that you own

unsavoury news about people we know

It is important to understand that there are differing expectations and norms of what small talk might entail. While culture can have an influence on how much small talk we should make and what topics are acceptable, individual personalities can also have an impact on one's view of small talk. In her book *Quiet*[1], American author Susan Cain suggests that introverts might feel more comfortable with in-depth conversations about topics like values and morality to more banal chat about the weather.

A good neutral starting point might be to comment on a mutual area of commonality, using it to elicit a response. For example, if you meet someone at a conference, you might comment on the location or the amazing keynote speech you had both been at (*'What a beautiful city! This is a great place for a conference!'*; *'That was a really interesting presentation.'*), or if you meet someone at a networking event or a party, you might talk about the delicious food or the incredible host (*'The open sandwiches are really tasty!'*; *'Dawn did really well putting this event together, didn't she?'*). Find something that you both have in common and keep your comments positive.

1 Cain Susan (2012) *Quiet: The power of introverts in a world that can't stop talking*. New York: Crown Publishers.

3 Encourage participation

Rather than spending the initial moments expanding on your opinions about a topic, find ways of inviting the other person into the conversation. There are many reasons why people might not voluntarily speak up: shyness, respect for their conversation partner, or a different turn-taking style are just some of them. However, people like to feel valued, and one way of showing someone that you value them is to encourage them to participate in conversation with you. After you've made your comment, ask for their opinion, e.g. *'That was a really interesting presentation. What did you think of it?'*; *'The open sandwiches are really tasty! Have you tried them?'*; *'Dawn did really well putting this event together, didn't she? Do you know Dawn?'*

4 Balance between questions and comments

It can be good to ask questions and encourage participation, but too many questions in a row can turn your first meeting into an interrogation and might intimidate your conversation partner. Too many statements and it might come across as a self-centred performance. Strike a balance between asking questions and responding to your partner. One way of doing this is to comment on what is being said, e.g. *'Wow, that's certainly interesting!'; 'I see what you mean'; 'I can't believe that happened to you!'*

5   Reveal something about yourself

You can also respond to your conversation partner by connecting what they've told you to a personal experience that you can share (*'Yes, this was a popular topic at the last conference I attended as well.'; 'Are you vegetarian? I tried being a vegetarian once. I did it for about two years before I went back to eating meat.'; 'I know, I've never organised an event like that, but I've supported my colleague in planning the office Christmas party and it wasn't easy.'*) By responding to your partner you are letting them know your thoughts, your opinions, your feelings, your beliefs and attitudes and who you really are.

In revealing something about yourself, you are not only showing a willingness to let your partner get to know you and demonstrating a certain level of trust, but you are also encouraging them to do the same. Be aware however of saying too much or sharing too much. You are, after all, still at the stage of making small talk, so keep the conversation light and leave the heavy stuff for when a deeper bond has been established. Also, be careful not to turn the conversation into a monologue (see previous tip).

6   Express curiosity and interest

Commenting on what is being said can also serve to demonstrate that you are actively listening. In your comments, you can:

- show your emotional response:
  'No way! That's incredible!', 'Really? That's amazing!'; 'That's not acceptable!'
- express your curiosity in what happened:
  'What happened after that?'; 'Did you really do that? How come no one else said anything?'
- express your curiosity in their feelings:
  'Did you enjoy that?'; 'Was that tough for you?'; 'How did you feel about that?'
- show solidarity:
  'I would be furious!'; 'Yes, we've all been there before.'; 'I know exactly what you mean. I had an experience like that once.'
- show an appreciation for their skills:
  'Wow, you've done a lot. I'd love to have that kind of experience.'; 'You handled that really well.'; 'That was such a great way of dealing with it. I wouldn't know what to do in that situation.'

7　Ask open-ended questions

A question that requires a *yes* or *no* answer such as, *'Are you vegetarian?'* or, *'Do you know Dawn?'* is known as a closed question. Such questions run the risk of your conversation abruptly ending with an awkward one-word answer, especially if your conversation partner subscribes to a culture where they are expected to answer only what is being asked and does not see the need to expand on what is being said. Couple your closed questions with open-ended ones that encourage your conversation partner to keep the conversation going, e.g. *'Why did you decide to become vegetarian?'*; *'How do you know Dawn?'*; *'How similar is that conference to this one?'*; *'What was the best part about that experience?'*

8　Keep your answers short and simple

While it's good to share something about yourself, trying to cram all the details and background of a story into an initial exchange could bore or overwhelm your conversation partner and might come across egotistical. Remember the useful acronym KISS (Keep It Short and Simple) and be efficient with your answer by keeping it short and simple.

> The next time you find yourself face to face with someone new, try using the ICE-BREAK model. Reflect on the encounter after the event and ask yourself these questions: Which stages did I find the easiest? What did I do that I normally wouldn't have done? What worked well and contributed to enhancing the interaction? Why?

Like with most things, the more practise we get, the better we become at making a good first impression.

Making first contact via email

Unfortunately, not all first encounters are face to face. While we might be able to get instant (verbal or non-verbal) feedback about the way we speak to someone in a face-to-face meeting, it might be trickier finding out how we are being perceived in an email exchange with someone we have never met.

**Consider the following email exchange.
What issues do you think might arise?**

To: Laura Constanza

Subject: Self-Introduction

Dear Ms Constanza,

I've recently taken over as the manager of Asian sales and wanted to introduce myself to you, seeing that I will be working closely with you and your marketing team in the near future.

My name is Cheng Shao Ting and I was previously marketing head of Simba International before moving to this company. I did my MBA at Columbia Business School in 2012 when I lived in New York for two years but have been mainly based in Shen Zhen for the last 20 years.

I'm looking forward to meeting you at the annual meeting in a few weeks.

Yours sincerely,
Cheng Shao Ting

To: Cheng Shao Ting

Subject: Re: Self-Introduction

Hi Shao Ting,

Thanks for your email. I read about your appointment in the company newsletter and really look forward to meeting you.

I hope you enjoy your new role.

Best,
Laura

In an attempt to come across as friendly and informal, Laura might have risked offending Mr Cheng. For Laura, it is common practice for her to begin all her emails with *'Hi'*, to address her recipients by their first names, to write short and succinct emails in order to respect the time of her recipient, and to sign off with 'Best', using her first name to signal how she would like to be addressed. However, a closer look at Mr. Cheng's more formal writing might have helped Laura consider how she could benefit from mirroring some of the features of his email, while still preserving some of her own style.

 In what ways does the following email mirror the writing style of Mr Cheng, and in what ways does Laura maintain a sense of her own style?

To: Cheng Shao Ting

Subject: Re: Self-Introduction

Dear Mr. Cheng,

Thank you for your email. I read about your appointment in the company newsletter and am looking forward to meeting you at our coming annual meeting.

I am intrigued by your self-introduction and would love to know more about your experience in New York. Before coming to YSA, I was working as an accounts executive for a company based in Manhattan. I was with them for four years before joining YSA in 2012.

I hope you enjoy your new role and I look forward to continuing our chat in person very soon.

Best regards,
Laura

 As Laura did not feel comfortable making a formal self-introduction over email, she used something that they both have in common i.e. New York, to say something about her past experience, thus reciprocating Shao Ting's self-introduction and allowing him to get to know her a little. Laura also adopted a slightly formal tone, addressing him with *'Dear Mr. Cheng'* instead of

'Hi Shao Ting', and using *'Thank you'* instead of *'Thanks'* and *'Best regards'* instead of *'Best'*. However, it was important to Laura that Shao Ting calls her by her first name as she found *Ms Constanza* too formal and too distant. In doing so, she was able to maintain her beliefs and values while accommodating Shao Ting's.

Have you ever received an email with a style completely different from your own? What was your first reaction? Did knowledge of their style have an influence on the way you responded to that email? What parts of your own style did you choose to preserve and why?

Socialising in business

I remember being called into an emergency intercultural skills workshop set up for a British company that was having problems getting a big Chinese client on board. It was a client they had been pursuing for over a year and they were getting nowhere near the signing of the contract. In our workshop, we brought up the idea of 'guanxi' i.e. relationships, something vital to doing business with the Chinese. For many Chinese business people, a relationship is based on trust, and this trust can only be built by getting to know the person not just in a professional context. It is therefore not uncommon for Chinese business people to spend most of their evenings going for dinner and having drinks with their colleagues and their business associates, strengthening a very personal bond and developing trust for their future business dealings.

Upon hearing this, the trainee sighed and said, *'We already know all that. But we just don't have the time. When we are in China we have more than 20 clients to see in that short trip. We can't just waste a whole day and evening on one client. Give us an easier way to develop this guanxi. Can we not just bring them an expensive gift or something?'*

Like many of us, the trainee had difficulty seeing past his own view of what was necessary to build trust between his company and the Chinese client. He believed that having a good business proposal with huge potential for profits, and some enthusiasm on his part, perhaps shown by his visit to China and the expensive gift, was enough to convince the Chinese client to sign the contract. Even when confronted with the fact that he needed to be spending time wining and dining his client, he still resisted, hoping for a quicker and easier option.

Below is another example of an Australian consultant, Ric, who found himself in a similar situation in Japan.

Consider what you might do if you found yourself in Ric's position. Why do you think Hiroshi was puzzled?

Ric was brought over from Sydney to Tokyo to consult on an engineering project. They were working long, intense hours in the day and Ric was exhausted. However, his Japanese team were keen to take him out for dinner and Karaoke in the evenings. Initially, he resisted their offers, stating that he was tired and needed some *'me time'*. One of his Japanese team members, Hiroshi, made a move to ask him what *'me time'* meant and Ric noticed the slightly puzzled expression on his face when he talked about privacy and having time to be alone. Hiroshi asked hesitantly, *'Why do you want to be alone? Do you not get lonely?'*

 It would have been easy for Ric to dismiss Hiroshi and his team as a bunch of workaholics who have no respect for his privacy or personal time. But Ric chose to engage Hiroshi in an open conversation about the topic instead. Read what happened to Ric and consider how he might have applied the ADAPT model that was presented in Chapter 2, page 45. Here's a reminder:

The ADAPT Model

 Consider how Ric is acting different from the way he was in the earlier project. What has changed, and how did Hiroshi feel as a result?

When they were talking about the concept of privacy, Hiroshi revealed that he grew up sharing a room with his three siblings. He still lived with his parents as he was not yet married, although he now had his own room. The only thing that separated Hiroshi's bedroom from the rest of the house was a thin paper door. Privacy wasn't something in Hiroshi's vocabulary, and he found the need for 'me time' novel and strange.

In an attempt to get his point across, Ric explained to Hiroshi that he has to be professional and behave in a business-like manner all day, and he needed the evening to be his non-business self and relax. It was then that Hiroshi exclaimed, *'Going out in the evenings is when you get to be your non-business self! And relax.'* Ric could see the benefits of team building over dinner, drinks and Karaoke, and reasoned with himself that it was a way for him to experience Japanese culture and have an insight into Japanese life. So Ric went along that night, and was surprised at how different his team members were behaving from their professional personas. Although there was some talk of work, most of the evening was spent sharing personal stories, making jokes and sometimes acting in a silly fashion. At the end of the evening, Hiroshi jokingly said to Ric, *'See? I know who you really are now!'*

Applying the ADAPT model: Ric realised that he was becoming annoyed at having to continue working in the evenings and continuing his professional role even during what should be his personal time. He became aware that there were differences between his and his team members' expectations of how the evenings should be spent. (**Awareness**). However, he withheld his judgments (**Don't judge**). and engaged in conversation with Hiroshi, finding out the reasons behind those differences. Ric realised that they had a different way of conceiving the boundary between what was professional and what was personal (**Analyse**). Ric convinced himself that it might help build up his team and give him a chance to experience Japanese life (**Persuade yourself**) and went out with his team that evening (**Try**).

Ric did not go out with his team every night of that week in Japan. He did however join them for half of his evenings there, and found that his attempt to integrate was very much appreciated by his team members. They were more able to open up to him at work and found value in their different ways of working. In giving a little and adapting his behaviour, Ric found that his team was also more willing to try and understand how he did things and adapt to him. Ric found a cultural mentor in Hiroshi and was able to go to him for open conversations to help Ric understand the differences in the way he (and his team) approached things.

While some of us might think that business and personal life should not mix, others might not see the boundary that clearly. While some of us might find it enough to trust someone based on their professional accomplishments and business arguments, others might feel the need to know someone on a more personal level in order to develop the trust required to do business together. While some might find it inappropriate to make small talk in a job interview, others might find small talk in an email a waste of time. We might have different ideas as to the part relationships should play in business. However, as we can see from the relationship/results circle (see 'The Relationships-Results Circle' on page 37), we need to be able to assess the different situations we are in and juggle the balance between the two in a way that works for all the parties involved.

Use of humour

In one of my training sessions, I once showed a TED talk in which the presenter, a serious academic, peppered his presentation with light-hearted humour and witticisms that had the audience breaking out in laughter. His presentation was full of thought-provoking messages but was also entertaining and palatable to the general public, the mark of a good speaker in the TED universe.

However, my trainees were divided on his use of humour. Some of them found it endearing, but to my surprise a large number of my trainees were unimpressed. One of them remarked, *'He was supposed to be presenting research but he was making so many jokes that I didn't think he was serious! Is he a comedian or an educator?'*

Comedies like Mr Bean are often used as examples of how universal humour can cross cultural boundaries, but play the buffoon like Mr Bean in your face-to-face interactions and you might find yourself in some awkward situations. Acting in a silly manner might be used by some to ease tensions and break the ice, but in countries like Japan and China, humour tends to be reserved for comedians and specialists in humour-related fields[25].

Laughter may be the best medicine for some, and sometimes it might be a great tool for building relationships, but it is not always universal. Some laugh to show solidarity and respect, whereas others laugh to diffuse a nervous situation. Some find laughter attractive, while others find that laughter makes them nervous and uncomfortable[26]. Some people might find it appropriate

---

25 Yue X, Jiang F, Lu S & Hiranandani N (2016) To be or not to be humorous? Cross-Cultural Perspectives on Humour. *Frontiers in Psychology* **7** 1495.

26 Liao CC (1998) *Jokes, Humor and Chinese People.* Taipei: Crane.

to make jokes at any time and any place, making light of serious things so as to make them seem less awful. Others prefer it if humour was reserved for certain occasions.

 Beth and Mina are colleagues. What do you think is happening here? What is Beth trying to do? How is Mina perceiving it?

Mina: *Beth, where's the stapler that was on my desk?*

Beth (with a deadpan face): *I ate it.*

Two days later ...

Beth: *... once you locate the paper jam, you pull the paper in the opposite direction and that should solve the problem.*

Mina: *Wow, where did you learnt to fix the photocopier?*

Beth (with a deadpan face): *Didn't you know? I have a degree in photocopying.*

Several days later ...

Mina: *I finally understand the British sense of humour. It's about bullying people.*

While Beth was using her specific brand of humour to bond with Mina, Mina was having trouble understanding Beth's jokes, interpreting them as Beth's way of taking a sarcastic dig at her and insulting her.

British anthropologist Kate Fox[1] notes that the English treat irony as 'a constant, a normal element of ordinary, everyday conversation' and the 'dominant ingredient in English humour'. However, the translation for 'irony' in both Japanese and Chinese also means sarcasm. Being ironic, therefore, could carry a negative connotation of insulting the hearer. What makes irony even more difficult for non-Brits to understand is the fact that delivering the joke with a deadpan face is the expected norm.

Another feature common to British humour is self-deprecation. In line with the British values of humility and modesty, one might hear a Brit putting themselves down or making themselves the butt of the joke in an attempt to bond with their counterparts. However, when communicating with people from other cultures, this behaviour might cause more confusion than intended.

---

1   Kate F (2004) *Watching the English.* London: Hodder and Stoughton.

Using humour

When communicating internationally, consider these six tips on using humour:

1 Avoid aggressive humour: humour that puts down, insults and pokes fun at your conversation partner. It is the type of humour used by bullies and is perceived negatively by most.

2 Avoid jokes that involve making fun at someone else's expense. This includes jokes that laughs at the stereotypes of a certain country, community or culture.

3 Listen and get a feel for your interlocutor's sense of humour. Try to adapt to it. You don't have to give up your own sense of humour but be sensitive to the differences.

4 Consider things that your interlocutor might relate to e.g. day-to-day challenges of the job or of home life, and find the comedy in situations (rather than people) to create a sense of fellowship.

5 Use irony sparingly in international communication and be aware that what might be lauded as wit in an English native speaker culture might just be seen as condescension and even one-upmanship to a non-native speaker.

6 Notice when it might be useful to add a 'Just joking!' to the end of your witty comment so that everyone involved is clear of your communication intent.

From the way we make small talk to the way we build relationships through socialising and our varied use of humour, we are influenced by the norms and expectations of our communities and also our individual tendencies. It is important that we don't assume that everyone operates in the same way as we do, and that we learn to pay attention to those little differences so as to build successful relationships across borders.

Chapter 4: Collaboration and teamwork

Being part of a diverse team

Christina was a British marketing manager for a global courier delivery services company based in the United States. When she was first put into an international team to work on a project aimed at generating new ideas and concepts for the company, she was excited about the variety and the new possibilities the different people on the team would bring. But, as time went by, Christina started to experience difficulties with the diversity. In a conversation with me she grumbled, '*I never thought people would play up to their stereotypes this much! Giovanni is always late for our virtual meetings, Claudia is a real stickler for detailed plans and schedules, Daniela is always so emotional and talks too much, and Junichi never says anything! It's so annoying. I just want to get things done, but there's never any clarity and all this to-ing and fro-ing is so unproductive!*'

Aside from the cultural differences, Christina also had to deal the challenges of communicating with her team virtually. This meant dealing with time differences, the lack of opportunities for social interactions and trust-building activities, and a missing sense of unity, commitment and common direction. Unfortunately, Christina is not alone in this feeling of frustration as more and more multinational corporations are moving towards team-based structures where staff members are placed in international teams to accomplish particular organisational goals.

International teams bring diverse skills, viewpoints, experiences and knowledge, which are extremely valuable. However, such diversity also brings with it a range of challenges. It is therefore even more important when working with international teams to ensure that all parties are on the same page and working towards the same goals, that they feel supported, informed and connected, and are able to develop a way of successfully communicating and understanding each other.

Communication styles

Whether you are collaborating with colleagues from a different department, with classmates on a school project, with friends to plan a joint holiday, or with family to organise a house move, the key to successful collaboration is effective communication. We often make assumptions about what the best and most appropriate way of communicating should be based on our own norms and expectations. It is therefore no surprise that communication issues are often listed as the number one problem when working in international teams. Tensions may rise and breakdowns in communication can occur if communication styles differ greatly within a team.

The first step to effective communication is to first become aware of your own communication style and your expectations and preferences in a conversation partner's communication style.

Our communication styles

 Look at the following communication styles. Where do you fall on the 14 different scales? You might find your style changing depending on the context or the people you are talking to, but where do you think your average style lies?

1. Without thinking about each one for more than five seconds, mark where you think you stand with an X on each scale.

   Complex --Simple

   Competitive -- Co-operative

   Concise answers ----------------------------------- Expansive answers

   Direct -- Indirect

   Distanced -- Close

   Emotional -- Factual

   Expressive --- Serious & contained

   Fast-paced --- Slow-paced

   Focused on details ---------------------------------- Focused on the big picture

   Passive --- Assertive

   Past-oriented -- Present/future-oriented

   Relationship-oriented ------------------------------- Task-oriented

   Silent listener -------------------------------------- Active listener

   Structured --- Flexible

2. How do you feel about your communication style? What do you like about it? Is there anything you'd like to change about it? What do you think others might think of your communication style?

3. Think about someone that you often have communication problems with. What might their communication style be like? Go back and mark an 'O' on each of the 14 scales based on where you think their style might lie.

4. Where are the differences between your communication styles? Where are the similarities? What do you think might be causing an issue with your interactions?

5. Now think about someone you collaborate well and enjoy working with. What might their communication style be like?

6. Go back and mark a ↓ on the scales based on where you think their style might lie.

7. What are the differences between the Os and the Xs? Are there any similarities?

8. How do you think you can adapt your communication style to better collaborate with the person in (3)?

Our communication style can be influenced by our upbringing, our education background, our life experiences, and the cultures of the communities we belong to. When faced with someone with a significantly different style from that which we are used to, we can sometimes jump to over-simplistic conclusions about that person. This is especially so in international communication.

How might the communication styles of Joe and Mia differ? How do you think Joe's assumptions (a) and (b) might affect their relationship?

Joe is finding it tiring working with Mia. He appreciates that Mia is full of enthusiasm for the project and likes to keep him informed of her progress. But every conversation seems to go on for a long time, with Mia giving Joe a lot of background information about her thoughts, her decision-making processes and her feelings about things. Even when it's Joe's turn to talk, Mia keeps interrupting with comments and questions. Joe figures this must be because (a) Mia is a woman and women like to talk a lot and/or (b) Mia is from Country A and people from Country A like to talk a lot.

While there might be an element of cross-cultural difference between Joe and Mia's communication styles, over-generalising could result in Joe feeling frustrated and powerless to improve their communications. By breaking down the elements of one's communication style, Joe would be better able to objectively understand that Mia has an expressive and emotional style of communication, prefers expansive answers and is an active listener, who uses comments and questions to demonstrate attention and interest. And these features of Mia's communication style might be due to a combination of cultural and individual personality factors.

Of course, it is also important to remember that it can be helpful both for the team and for ourselves to work with people with a different communication style from our own. Not only would they be able to add a different perspective on the issues faced, they might also prompt us to reflect on the advantages and disadvantages of our own communication style, and inspire us to consider ways of adapting the way we communicate in order to suit the context and situations we find ourselves in.

The DISC Model

A tool that can help frame our understanding of communication styles is the DISC model. Originally conceived by American psychologist William Marston in the 1920s, and later developed into a behavioural assessment tool by organisational psychologist Walter Clarke, the DISC model is commonly used in companies when hiring, appraising and developing their staff. It categorises people's behaviour and communication styles into four types, often illustrated by a disc-like diagram as seen on page 69.

Each quadrant represents a different trait:

- **Dominance:** A person in this quadrant is a confident driver of communication who is results- and goal-oriented, decisive, fast-paced, competitive and tends to get straight to the point when communicating.
- **Influence:** A person in this quadrant is sociable and enjoys sharing and working in teams, is optimistic, demonstrative, entertaining and open. They tend to be expansive and can go off track when speaking.
- **Steadiness:** A person in this quadrant is dependable, calm, sincere, attentive and supportive. They tend to be slow-paced and methodical in the way they communicate.

● **Conscientiousness:** A person in this quadrant is analytical, cautious and results-oriented. They value expertise, accuracy and precision. They tend to communicate in a slow-paced, direct and factual way.

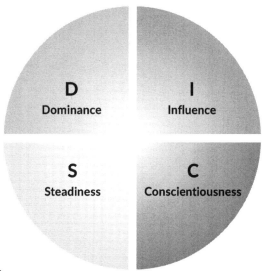

The DISC Model

 Consider communication styles, using the DISC Model for reference

1. When communicating with someone, look for cues to help you identify their communication style. Do they speak quickly (D & I)? Do they seem very focused on the task (D & C)? Do they talk about emotions (I & S)? Do they seem methodical and systematic (S & C)?

2. Where in the DISC model would you place yourself? Are you mostly D (Dominant) with some I (Influencing) tendencies? Are you sometimes an S (Steady) and sometimes a C (Conscientious)? Are you a little bit of everything depending on the situation you are in and the people you are talking to?

An awareness of how you and your conversation partners prefer to communicate can make a huge difference to how you perceive the interaction and how successful it is. To ensure effective communication and successful relationship building, we sometimes need to go beyond simply knowing their communication style and try to adjust our own style of communication so as to accommodate and adapt to our conversation partner.

Adapting our communication style

Insert the following headings into the correct gap

Dominant   Influencing   Steady   Conscientious

A. Communicating with the .... type	B. Communicating with the .... type
● Allow thinking time and listen. ● Provide facts and details. ● Establish your credibility but don't act like an expert if you're not. ● Be structured and systematic. ● Use old routines and frameworks to warm them to new ideas. ● Avoid putting pressure on them for action.	● Show admiration for them. ● Get to your point quickly. ● Allow them to lead and take control of the conversation. ● Be structured and systematic. ● Avoid deviating from the topic. ● Demonstrate your competence.
C. Communicating with the .... type	D. Communicating with the .... type
● Show that you are interested in them. ● Ask for help or support. ● Express support and appreciation. ● Ensure there is clarity in what is expected and what is to be done. ● Create a safe and warm atmosphere. ● Give them time to adjust to changes. ● Avoid confrontation.	● Use praise and show recognition for achievements. ● Be relaxed and sociable. ● Value small talk. ● Smile. ● Show emotions. ● Turn what you want to say into a story. ● Avoid going into too much detail.

Answers: A Conscientious; B Dominant; C Steady; D Influencing.

💬 Understanding DISC in different discourses: While some of us might be a C (conscientious) at the office, we might take on D (dominant) characteristics at home when dealing with our children and S (steady) behavioural inclinations when hanging out with our friends on a social evening. An individual can take on a variety of communication styles depending on the context, the role they are playing, and the way they might see themselves in relation to the people they are talking to. The cultural norms of a community can also play a part. The following critical incident demonstrates how overgeneralising someone's communication style can sometimes have unintended results.

What might go wrong with Sara's attempt at adapting and accommodating to Ken's perceived style?

After working virtually with Ken for six months, Sara has just met him face-to-face for the first time at a team networking event. Ken is very animated as he chats to Sara, telling her stories about the people from his country and being quite open about his opinions and feelings. Sara believes this must mean Ken is an Influencer according to the DISC model she had just been reading about. She starts to make constant eye contact, makes jokes about the people at the party and gets quite talkative.

How might considering the following help Sara?

● how eye contact might be seen in some cultures

● how humour can differ across cultures

● how gender expectations might differ across cultures.

To some, eye contact might indicate that you are paying attention, while to others, it is a sign of flirting and sexual attraction. In the West, eye contact is often related to confidence, openness and honesty. However, in countries like Japan and Nigeria, direct eye contact can be interpreted as disrespect (→ see Chapter 10 for more on this.)

The use of humour to build relationships can also have undesirable outcomes, especially when it involves saying negative things about others (→ see Chapter 3). Combined with the fact that Ken might not have expected a woman to talk to him in such a gregarious and assertive fashion, Sara's attempt to match Ken's influencing communication style without careful attention to the other factors did not go down too well. Ken came away thinking Sara was boisterous, aggressive and mean-spirited.

Applying the DISC model or any communication model or framework blindly could result in undesirable consequences. While we cannot be expected to know the cultural expectations of every individual, we can train ourselves to be more sensitive to the reactions we are getting to our communication style, to be aware of the possible areas of miscommunication, to reflect on the reasons why our style might not be working, and to find a way that works for the people that we are communicating with.

If you sense that differences in communication styles are causing an issue and/or there is a possibility of a misunderstanding

> happening, it can sometimes be helpful to have an open conversation about the way communication takes place. Where possible, have your team look at the communication styles and the DISC model detailed in this chapter. As a group, focus on raising awareness of the way each individual of the team prefers to communicate and discuss how communication might work best for the team. There is no better way of working through communication issues than taking time to communicate about communicating.

Time

This chapter began with Christina voicing her frustration with how some of her team members had different ideas as to how time was best utilised. Often on international projects, members are working under time constraints and any activity that is seen as a waste of time could be perceived as a sign of disrespect, or simply a lack of professionalism.

Consider Christina's situation again. From her point of view, in what ways is each of her team members wasting time? Write down her possible assumptions in the gaps below. The first one has been done for you as an example.

A. Giovanni is always late for our virtual meetings

Being late for meetings is a waste of everyone's time. It's not fair to everyone else who's punctual. It's unproductive spending time filling Giovanni in on things that he's missed.

B. Claudia is a real stickler for detailed plans and schedules

C. Daniela is always so emotional and talks too much

D. Junichi never says anything!

Did your answers look something like this?

B Over-planning and drawing up detailed plans is a waste of time because we don't know what's going to work or not. It's better to just act on it, and leave enough flexibility for changes.

C Talking too much and dwelling on emotions is a waste of time. It's more efficient to stick to the facts and keep what we need to say concise.

D Not saying anything is a waste of everyone's time. Junichi is not contributing to the group and people have to guess what he thinks of things. Clarity is key and such ambiguity isn't productive.

Obviously, most team members do not set out to waste their group's time. They act in the way they think is best, and certain beliefs and values underlie their actions. Christina, however, has not left much room for other interpretations aside from her own.

Using the ADAPT model from Chapter 2 (page 45) (Awareness-Don't Judge-Analyse-Persuade Yourself-Try), Christina became aware of her own assumptions. She realised that she was reacting in that way because she was focused on being efficient and getting things done, and because she believed that nothing is gained by talking about the same things over and over. She pushed aside her judgments and analysed the reasons for her group members' behaviours by doing some research and reading up on intercultural communication issues. She then started an open dialogue with her individual teammates about the issues she was having.

Analyse Christina's statements in box above again. What other interpretations might you find? Are they the same as the ones Christina discovered below?

A. Giovanni is always late for our virtual meetings.
He seems to expect everyone to arrive at meetings 15-20 minutes late because that is how meetings operate in his local office. He thought that coming on time would be a waste of his time because he'd be the only one there.

B. Claudia is a real stickler for detailed plans and schedules.
She believes that detailed plans and schedules are a way of saving time. By spending a bit more time at the planning stage and have a clear view of what is to come, she can then anticipate any setbacks and deal with them more efficiently when they do happen. She feels that not planning thoroughly will result in a waste of time.

C. Daniela is always so emotional and talks too much.
She believes that it is important to express one's thoughts and emotions as it prevents team members from harbouring bad feelings, which can affect team morale. Being open and honest can not only improve communication but can enable team members to truly get to know each other, something that can be difficult to do virtually.

D. Junichi never says anything!
He finds it necessary to listen and think about what is being said carefully before responding to it. To him, rash responses can lead to bad feelings, which can affect team morale. When there's disagreement involved, he is reluctant to cause any loss of face for his colleagues (see → *'Face', on page 75) and prefers to be indirect about his opinions, perhaps dealing with it in a later email.*

With a better understanding of the reasons behind her team members' behaviour, Christina started to think about how she could align herself in order to better work with them. She found herself agreeing with the benefit of planning ahead and anticipating problems, and she also saw the importance of being true to herself and expressing her opinions with her teammates. She succeeded in persuading herself to try adapting slightly to Claudia and Daniel's ways of working instead of being focused on rushing the project to action.

Christina could understand Junichi's point of view and decided to respect his need for thinking time and space. In talking to him about the issue, he started reflecting on the need to perhaps be more direct with his communication. Talking openly about time with Giovanni also had an effect on his punctuality. Upon realising that his other teammates were always waiting for him, he started arriving to meetings on time.

Considerations of time

❶ Like Christina, some people have a relatively linear view of time. Things are seen as taking place chronologically one after the other, and there is a focus on being efficient and getting things done. It is important to note that not everybody sees time in the same way. Those from a flexible time culture might not experience time as such a finite resource. Multiple things can happen at the same time, things overlap and are dealt with when they arise. Changes are to be expected and flexibility is key.

❷ Some people have a short-term orientation to time with a focus on the past and the present, preferring to leave things the way it has always been. They might be resistant to new ideas, saying things like, *'But that's not how we do things here'*. Others might have a more long-term orientation to time, with a focus on working hard for the future.

❸ Everyone works to their own set of rules when it comes to time. Drawing on Christina's example, some see the start time of a meeting as the time participants are expected to arrive, others expect the meeting to start 10, 20 or even 30 minutes later than the stated time and so arrive accordingly. The same applies to task deadlines and email response times. It would be helpful for team leaders to have an open conversation with their members at the start of a project to clarify expectations.

❹ Working with international teams often means dealing with time differences. Very often synchronous meetings are arranged according to the time zone of the project leader or the company headquarters. Having to wake up at 3am for virtual meetings on a regular basis can result in some very disgruntled team members. Consider discussing this with your team and finding a group solution to this issue.

Face

The concept of face is a difficult one to define. Words like *dignity, prestige*, and *public image* have been used to describe it, but it is a concept most easily understood when we consider the notion of *losing face*: i.e. being humiliated in front of others, thus resulting in a possible loss of their respect. Although often associated with the Chinese term *mianzi*, the concept of face can be found in many different languages, from Arabic to Slavic to Thai. These cultures seem to share an understanding of a social dignity that, if lost in front of others, would cause us great embarrassment.

While we can argue that no one would want to be humiliated or embarrassed, the events that can cause a loss of face could differ from culture to culture.

Imagine yourself in the ten situations below. Which ones would you consider to be a loss of face for you? Which ones would upset and worry you?

1. You make a proposal in a meeting and one of your colleagues openly questions something you said and starts to debate it.

2. You are chairing a meeting and one of your subordinates openly disagrees with you.

3. You invite your colleague out for dinner and in front of the other staff, he tells you that he can't because he has to get home for dinner that day.

4. You quote the wrong statistic in a negotiation and your manager tells you off in front of your clients.

5. You lose out on an important client to a competing colleague and she tells everyone in the office.

6. A subordinate asks you a question in front of the others and you do not know the answer.

7. All your colleagues seem to have heard about the new policy changes except you.

8. Everyone in the office seems to have got the newest smart phone except you.

9. In a meeting, everyone in your team receives praise for doing their job well, except you.

10. In a meeting, you alone receive a lot of praise in front of your colleagues, who do not look particularly pleased.

Not all of the ten scenarios above might bother you, but you cannot assume that what doesn't upset you will not upset others. Undoubtedly, what we might consider a loss of face differs, and how much sleep we lose over it might also vary from person to person and culture to culture. It is important that we are mindful of the sensitivities of our teammates and avoid embarrassing someone, especially when we are aware of how much that might mean to that individual.

An awareness of potential incidents that might make someone lose face could help us be more sensitive to our teammates and co-workers, and as a result help us to build and maintain trust in our relationships. Furthermore, this is an awareness that can be built through research (reading books like this one), observations, a keenness to reflect on our experiences, and a willingness to openly discuss these questions.

With that in mind, we could explore ways of 'giving face' to others so as to cultivate our relationships and build team cohesion. Although the responsibility of developing trust (see → 'Trust', on page 78) within a team often falls to the team leader, a team that gets along and works well together benefits everyone involved. Each team member therefore has the duty of working towards better collaboration and teamwork.

Behaviour in teams

Here are some examples of how team leaders and participants of international teams can adapt their behaviour to 'give face' to their teammates.

- Ensuring that each team member is given a chance to speak in meetings.

- Ensuring that each team member knows they are being heard by acknowledging and commenting on what is said (in person or via email).

- Recognising effort and achievement and voicing appreciation on a regular basis, but being sensitive about singling people out.

- Being sensitive when pointing out mistakes in front of others. Consider if it is necessary to point out the mistake there and then, or if you could do it in a more private setting.

- Being sensitive when refusing invitations, tasks, etc.

- Considering the way you voice disagreement and separate the facts from the person. Not agreeing with a decision does not equate not liking the decision-maker.

- Not shouting, making personal attacks or getting into emotional disagreements in front of others.

- Being aware of the geographical locations, skills and cultural backgrounds of the majority of the team and being careful not to neglect the minority.

- Not leaving anyone out where possible.

- Being aware of the English levels of all involved and not making anyone feel incompetent and embarrassed by their lack of language ability.

Trust

Collaboration cannot take place without trust. Trust is what holds a team together and enables them to work effectively and efficiently towards the same goals. Trust is often a huge part of building and maintaining relationships, and allows us to rely on that person, believing that they have our best interests at heart. A lack of trust can, however, lead to fear, suspicion and a breakdown in the relationship.

> **How is each team member attempting to foster an environment of trust? What might Vanessa think of what her team members were doing? What might her team members think of what Vanessa is doing?**
>
> When Vanessa was appointed team leader, one of the first things she did was to organise a team-building lunch at the nearby restaurant. Her team responded very positively to the idea and all turned up with enthusiasm. During the lunch, Vanessa made sure that everyone felt comfortable and had their tastes catered for. She told them about her family and showed them photos of her children, sharing some personal details about the things she loves and the day-to-day chores that she finds challenging.
>
> When the conversation turned to Pat, she started talking about her educational background, the topic of her dissertation, and the things she had learnt from her previous job. Mark seemed interested in the processes examined in Pat's MBA and asked her some questions before talking about how he applied the same processes to his previous project and achieved amazing results. Ron joined in, talking about the importance of finding the right process for the team. Referring to his experience that led to the closing of a billion-dollar contract, Ron talked about how his expertise in international negotiation could add value to the team. Vanessa's attempt to bring the topic back to family and hobbies was politely brushed off.

💬 Although it seemed like Vanessa and her team were on different pages, they all saw the lunch as an opportunity to build trust with their new team mates. Vanessa and her team members however had a different vision of how trust in a team should be built, and this might have led to very different impressions of each other's methods. Vanessa might have thought that Pat, Mark and Ron were being competitive and boastful of their own accomplishments while she prioritised building trust by being caring, authentic and open about the different sides of herself. Pat instead tried to build trust by demonstrating her knowledge through her education history and qualifications, while Mark and Ron were keen to gain trust by letting everyone know about their skills, their experience and their previous performance in business. Vanessa's team might have perceived her approach as being too intimate, weak and even unprofessional.

Richard Barrett, author, speaker and thought leader on the evolution of human values in business and society, suggests that the principle components of trust are character and competence. Character is made up of intent and integrity and generally reflects how you are on the inside. Competence on the other hand reflects how you are on the outside and can be further broken down into one's capability and the results one obtains. Barrett's trust matrix elaborates on how these components of trust are usually demonstrated.

The Trust Matrix

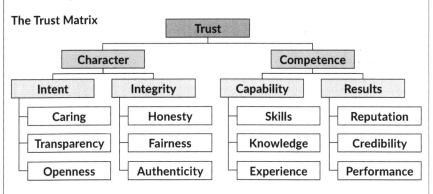

By engaging team members in an open dialogue about trust, we can not only clearly see which elements of trust are present or missing, but we can also better understand the different approaches to trust-building and the different priorities we might have when building relationships with the people that we work with.

Transparency

When communicating with others, most people have a tendency to assume that other people are privy to what is going on in their own heads. After all, we know what we mean, so others must know what we mean too. This phenomenon is known to psychologists as 'the illusion of transparency', and is the cause of multiple communication breakdowns.

In the previous critical incident, Vanessa had expected her team members to know that the lunch was for getting to know each other on a more personal and private level. Having the illusion of transparency, Vanessa had presumed that they shared her understanding of what team building meant. Pat, Mark and Ron, however, had a very different interpretation of what the lunch should entail and were surprised that Vanessa was not on the same page.

When collaborating internationally, incidents like Vanessa's team-building lunch very often get ignored. Personality differences are blamed for a lack of mutual understanding and rifts are deepened, making collaboration difficult.

 Improving teamwork

When working in international teams, consider the following ten tips for increased transparency and greater teamwork:

❶ Get to know each other as individuals, both on a professional and a personal level. Find out what motivates your team mates, what they are interested in, what they are good at, etc. Get to know their communication styles and how they like to collaborate. Team leaders on virtual teams might want to consider how they might get their team to bond and incorporate casual 'get-to-know-you' chats in online communications.

❷ Don't assume that you know what other team members mean. If unsure, ask questions and clarify.

❸ Adopt a modest attitude and be ready to learn from your team mates. Team leaders could benefit from fostering an atmosphere where team members are happy to learn from each other.

❹ Offer constructive feedback and accept feedback graciously. Feedback should be seen as a way for the team to move forward. Team leaders should ask for input on how they are doing and create appropriate channels for feedback to take place.

❺ Avoid an 'us versus them' attitude developing within your team, especially when a large number of team members come from a certain department or geographical location. Team leaders should work on creating an inclusive team culture and build a shared team identity.

❻ Communicate about communicating. In your initial meetings, negotiate with the team regarding how they would like to communicate. Who should they turn to when there are issues to be resolved? What medium of communication should be used? Who should be copied into such communication? Have regular updates on the communication processes in the team: are the existing processes working? What is unclear? What could be improved?

❼ Be open and do not be afraid of disagreement. Not all disagreement is a personal attack. Learn to separate your emotional reactions from your professional ones. Team leaders could cultivate a team that is open to expressions of ideas and opinions, and regularly emphasise that every idea or opinion is valid and worthwhile.

❽ Remember your overall goals. Why have you been put in this team? What do you want to achieve from this collaboration? Team leaders should communicate the goals and timelines of the team clearly, and regularly ensure that those goals are shared by all team members.

❾ Anticipate possible issues that could arise due to cultural differences or differences in expectations, and have open conversations about what is acceptable or appropriate for your team.

❿ Keep in contact with your team leader and team mates. Team leaders need to ensure that team members are given the channels to contribute and schedule regular meetings to keep them informed of the latest updates and their roles in the bigger scheme of things.

In the following chapter we'll explore issues with communication in greater detail.

Chapter 5: Getting the right message

As seen in 'Communication styles' on page 66 of Chapter 4, there are many different styles of communicating and if someone communicates in a way we are not used to, it might result in miscommunication and misunderstandings. Concepts like 'directness', 'politeness' and 'uncertainty avoidance' could enable us to categorise broadly how someone communicates, but they could also lead to over-generalisations and oversimplification of issues. After all, indirectness can be expressed in numerous different ways, politeness can be extremely subjective, and uncertainty avoidance, like everything else, is completely relative.

Through the topics of directness, politeness and uncertainty avoidance, this chapter hopes to explore the complexity of these issues and encourage a better awareness of how we communicate and how we can improve our understanding (and spot misunderstandings) when we are trying to get the right messages across.

Directness

I had always seen myself as a direct kind of person. I took pride in saying what I meant, I was not afraid of confrontation and I didn't mince my words. Growing up in Singapore, we were used to being efficient with words, dropping the superfluous modal verbs and adverbs when speaking, preferring a more direct, *'Who called?'* as opposed to, *'May I know who was calling for me?'* The short, clipped sentences and staccato tones of Singaporean English perhaps also contributed to my impression that Singaporeans spoke in a direct way.

When I first arrived in the UK in my early 20s, I was warned that the British were extremely indirect, and that what was said could be quite different from what was meant. I soon realised that invitations to, *'Come over for dinner some time!'* were never really followed through, that hedging and vague language was a norm (*It's quite nice; It's kind of cold; It's probably true*), and that negatives were often used to cushion a criticism (*It's not very big; It's not the most effective way; He's not exactly Einstein*). A trip to the local bookstore (or a quick online search) would uncover several comic strips, dictionaries and tables that compare what the British say to what they really mean. *That's not bad* actually means *That's really good*; *That's a very brave proposal!* probably means *That's an insane idea!* and *I'm a little bit disappointed that ...* should be understood as *I am annoyed that ...*

When my manager in London handed out my very first rota for a teaching job in a school I had been trying to get a job in for a while, I immediately noticed that one of my shifts coincided with my best friend's wedding. Not wanting to offend the manager who had just hired me, I said, *'This is great. You can see so clearly at a glance who's on duty on each day. And, look, that Tuesday is the day my best friend is getting married!'* My manager smiled and remarked, *'Great'.* I carried on, *'They've been planning this wedding for years and they're finally getting married here in London'.* He looked at me and said, *'You must be so happy for them'.*

I was sure I had been quite direct with him (taking the lessons learnt earlier into account) and that he had got the message but the revision of the rota I was hoping for never came. I never brought up the subject again and ended up missing my best friend's wedding.

Occurrences like this one kept happening to me over the years and I attributed them to everything but the (in)directness of my communication style. Whenever I made a suggestion or gave an opinion in a group discussion, it felt to me that I was being ignored. It did not occur to me that I was being too indirect and that the people around me hadn't picked up on my suggestions or intentions. It also seemed unimaginable then that the British, who were supposed to be masters at indirectness, would be unable to understand indirect communication.

One day I was writing an email asking my manager for time off and showed it to my British colleague Tim, who remarked that I was being extremely unclear.

Although this is not the exact copy, here is a sample of the email I wrote. How direct/indirect do you think I was? What assumptions was I making? How clear was my message?

To: Belinda Miles	**Date:** 5th January
Subject: Belinda Miles	

I hope you are well and enjoying the fresh snow that this week has brought. My housemates and I have been building snowmen in our garden but our hands always get too cold.

Thank you for mentoring my diploma thesis. You might be pleased to know that I've been working hard at nights finishing the second draft. I'm hoping that it'll be done by mid-February and we can have that celebratory drink we've been talking about.

As you know, I'm teaching an exam class this month. It's a pity because Chinese New Year falls on next Wednesday the 14th January and we usually put on our best clothes and welcome visitors to our home that day. Chinese New Year eve is also a day of celebration. That's when we normally have our reunion dinner with our family members, not unlike the Christmas dinners in the UK. The students' exam is on Monday the 19th January so once that is over, the students will be more relaxed. Chinese New Year is normally celebrated for 15 days and so having the 21st and 22nd to work on my thesis would mean that it still wouldn't be too late to have a celebration with my housemates.

Thank you for your kind attention.

Best regards,
Chia

In my mind, I was being very clear. I wanted some time off on the 21st and 22nd January and I was giving my line manager enough background information and reasons to approve my request. Surprised by Tim's comment, I asked him to look at my email again and point out exactly where he thought I was not being clear. He felt I was being *vague* and was making my request in an ambiguous way that required too much mental energy to decipher.

'But isn't indirectness good? The British are all about being indirect, aren't they?' I exclaimed. Tim sighed and said, 'Yes, and no. The British can be indirect, but not in emails like this. Managers don't have time to decipher emails like that. You need to get to the point'. It was then I realised that the terms *direct* and *indirect* might be too sweeping a generalisation to describe the communication style of a culture.

High and low context communication

First introduced by Edward T Hall in 1976, the cultural dimension of high versus low context communication (see → 'Cultural frameworks and dimensions' on page 33) has often been over-simply defined as indirect versus direct communication. Upon closer investigation, the *indirectness* described in *high context communication* is not the same as the indirectness of the British, described above. The use of shared context and the emphasis on relationships defined high context communication in a way that seemed to describe how I had been communicating.

Below is a table expanding on the differences between high and low context cultures. Can you match features of my email above to the features of high context communication in the table below?

High context communication	Low context communication
● The context, the situation and shared knowledge are often used to interpret meaning. The message is more implicit and might require the recipient to read between the lines. ● Information is given from general to specific. Background information is important to a better understanding of the situation. One often talks around the point. ● The message and the relationship one has with the recipient are connected. ● Communication is seen as a way of building relationships.	● Meaning is often carried by what is said and the message is more explicit. ● Information starts with the specific and moves towards the general. The point is made clearly and efficiently. Speed is valued. ● The message is often associated with the end goal. There is focus on the task and what needs to be done. ● Communication is seen as a way to exchange information, ideas and opinions.

My email turned out to be the epitome of high context communication, with the following high context features:

- Personal details that would enable the manager to get to know me better and improve rapport, e.g. '... enjoying the fresh snow'.

- Recognition of the manager's support and help, e.g. 'Thank you for mentoring ...'

- Demonstrations of hard work and an assumption that this is a desired trait in an employee and equates reliability, e.g. 'I've been working hard at nights'.

- References to previous chat, e.g. 'that celebratory drink we've been talking about'.

- Detailed background information about why the time off is needed, e.g. 'we usually put on our best clothes and welcome visitors to our home that day. Chinese New Year eve is also a day of celebration...'.

- An assumption that the recipient can see from my message that Chinese New Year is an important day for me and that I would like to have the day off that day.

- An assumption that the recipient understands that students might not come to class on the days after their exam from the statement 'once it is over, students will be more relaxed'.

- An assumption that the recipient would be able to read into my request to take 21st and 22nd January off work to focus on my thesis and celebrate Chinese New Year.

High context communication is often associated with East Asian and Arabic cultures and low context communication tends to be associated with more Anglo-Saxon (e.g. German, British, American) and Scandinavian cultures. Although the efficiency of Singaporean's use of English could be interpreted as a form of direct communication, there are many elements of high context communication in the way Singaporeans communicate that could be seen as indirect: the background information given when making a point, the use of shared knowledge and nonverbal cues, and the focus on relationship building and not just the key message. And the influence of my upbringing might have inherently influenced my style of communication, which, unbeknownst to me, had been the root of my communication issues. Directness clearly had more than one face and I had made the mistake of oversimplifying the concept.

Adapting to high or low context communication

Although high and low context communication is often discussed in relation to national culture, most of us are not exclusively high or low context in our communication style. We each employ a range of low- or high- context communication features depending on the context and the people we are talking to. Many of us would use high context communication when speaking to our friends and family but might opt for low context communication when we need to get the message across in order to get things done quickly.

If you are applying a low context communication style and encounter someone with a high context communication style, what might you do to persuade yourself to adapt? (See ➜ P for Persuade of the ADAPT model on page 45.) Consider the situations where you are more high context: e.g. when talking to colleagues you see as friends; when chatting over lunch; when going out for drinks in the evenings. Now consider how you are able to shift your communication style to adapt to your conversation partner. Instead of a supplier, could you see yourself as a long-term business acquaintance? Instead of his manager, could you see yourself as his mentor or even big brother? Would it help to change the setting e.g. take your conversation partner out of the office building and go for lunch or for drinks?

Conversely, if you are applying a high context communication style and encounter someone who is being low context, consider situations where you might be less focused on the relationship and more concerned about the agenda and the efficiency of communication e.g. when you are under a deadline and need specific information to proceed with your task; when you are 24 hours away from the important event you are organising and you need your staff to co-operate and get things done; when you are talking to a post office manager about a complex delivery request you have. Think about your behaviour and your communication style when playing those roles. How can you apply this to the way you communicate with your low context conversation partner?

Our different cultures might affect when and where we see high or low context communication as acceptable and appropriate. Our context and conversation partners may also have a huge part to play in the communication styles we take on. By being aware of the different roles we take on when communicating with the different people in our lives, we are able to be more flexible and adapt our communication style to the people we are communicating with.

Politeness

During a visit to a friend's village pub in Spain, I decided I was going to put my basic Spanish to use and order myself a beer. Translating the sentence, *'Can I have a beer please?'* in my head, I walked to the bar and made what I thought was a polite request, *'¿Puedo haber una cerveza porfavor?'*

To my surprise, the Spanish bar man looked at me suspiciously and proceeded to pour my beer with a frown on his face. My Spanish friend, upon hearing my request, ran up and interjected, saying, *'Just say, "a beer please!"*: *"¡una cerveza por favor!"'* It turns out that in Spanish bars, people don't make requests by saying *'Can/Could I ...?'* and attempting to do so made me come across as dubious and odd rather than polite.

In the English language, the indirectness of a request is often seen as a measure of politeness, as seen in the diagram below.

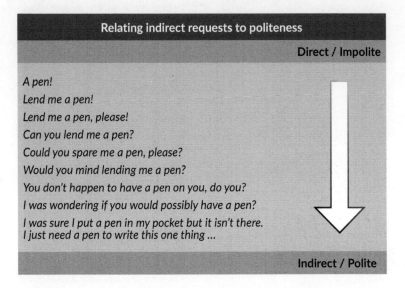

Relating indirect requests to politeness
Direct / Impolite
A pen!
Lend me a pen!
Lend me a pen, please!
Can you lend me a pen?
Could you spare me a pen, please?
Would you mind lending me a pen?
You don't happen to have a pen on you, do you?
I was wondering if you would possibly have a pen?
I was sure I put a pen in my pocket but it isn't there.
I just need a pen to write this one thing ...
Indirect / Polite

The regular use of indirect formulaic phrases like, *'Would you mind ...'* and, *'I was wondering if you could ...'* means that they are immediately interpreted as polite requests when used in English-speaking countries. However, the same formulas do not necessarily apply to other languages and other cultures (as seen in my experience of the Spanish pub), nor is indirectness always associated with politeness either.

American Linguist Robin Lakoff stated that we use politeness to reduce friction in our interactions and equated polite behaviour with being friendly, not imposing on others, and making our conversation partners feel good[27]. The definition of politeness, however, can differ greatly depending on the culture: some cultures define politeness as being friendly; others define it as being cultivated, considerate, respectful, or even self-effacing[28]. What is considered socially appropriate in one culture might not be so in another, and very often ignorance about the norms of one culture could result in behaviour that might be perceived as being impolite.

27   Lakoff R (1973) The logic of politeness: minding your p's and q's. *Chicago Linguistics Society* **8** pp292–305.

28 Watts R (2003) *Politeness.* Cambridge: Cambridge University Press.

Consider the situations below and decide if you would mark the behaviour described as (a), (b) or (c).

	a = Polite b = Acceptable c = Impolite and inappropriate	
1	Your colleague changes the topic when you ask her about her family.	
2	A supplier writes an email to you with a request regarding something that is not your responsibility and you don't reply.	
3	You take your business associates out for a meal and instead of letting you do the ordering, they each tell you what they would like to eat.	
4	Your host takes you out for a drink and after a few hours of drinking, you refuse their offer to pour you yet another drink.	
5	Your supplier's colleague has made a mistake with your order. Your supplier acknowledges the mistake but does not apologise for it.	
6	As team leader, you write to a team member for a progress update but he doesn't reply for more than 24 hours.	
7	Your client video calls you without any advance warning.	
8	One of your employees emails his clients and takes phone calls during department meetings.	

Look back at the responses you have given above and consider the assumptions you made when giving those answers. Now, consider the following norms that might have led to the above behaviour:

1   For some, small talk about one's family and personal life is part of building trust in a relationship. Others might prefer to keep their work and private lives separate.

2   For some, correspondence that requires action that is not within the receiver's knowledge or responsibility do not need a response. For others, acknowledgement of the email is necessary.

3   In more collectivist cultures with a higher power distance (see → 'Cultural frameworks and dimensions' on page 33), it is the norm for the host or the one who makes the invitation to decide what food should be ordered. In others, the individual gets to decide what they would like to order for themselves.

4   Some might see an outright refusal as a face-taking act (see → 'Dealing with Intercultural Communication' on page 43). Others might see such honesty as acceptable.

5   In some cultures, apologies are seen as a personal admittance of fault and an acceptance of blame and responsibility and are therefore avoided. In others, apologies are seen as a way of showing sympathy and remorse and a way of repairing trust. As such, apologies on behalf of one's company, colleagues or family are more common and expected.

6   While some expect replies to emails to take no longer than 24 hours, others might tolerate longer response periods. When working with a new team, it is important to establish an expected timeframe for such communication.

7   The protocol for a new media like video chats and other forms of electronic communication might differ from company to company, person to person. It is therefore useful to openly communicate about the expectations and the ways electronic communication is conducted.

8   For those with a more linear view of time (see → 'Cultural frameworks and dimensions' on page 33 and 'Intercultural competence' on page 39), there is an expectation that things are done one at a time. When a meeting is happening, our focus should be entirely on the meeting. For those with a more flexible view of time, multi-tasking might be the norm. Again, it is key that teams communicate what is expected and establish their own rules, rather than assuming that every participant knows and operates by the same rules.

Politeness is often a matter of perception and largely associated with the conventions we are used to. It is also highly dependent on context and the relationships we have with the people we interact with. Although it might seem polite to borrow a pen from a stranger at a bus-stop with an utterance like, *'I was wondering if you might possibly have a pen,'* the same utterance might come across sarcastic if you were talking to a husband you'd been married to for 50 years, and it might make you seem rather strange if you were asking for a pen at a stationery shop.

Before making assumptions about how impolite or rude someone is, it is important to take a step back and consider how they might be operating according to a different set of conventions and expectations. And don't forget to ask yourself what YOU might be doing that could be considered rude. After all, mismatched perceptions can easily skew our understanding of the intended message.

Uncertainty avoidance

James moved from New Zealand to Egypt to start a new job and started Arabic classes to equip himself with the local language. During his class, his Arabic teacher taught him the phrase *Inshallah* and summarised it to mean *Probably*. More accurately, *Inshallah* means *God willing* and signifies the speaker's wish for a particular event to occur, but in an attempt to keep things simple in James's elementary Arabic class, the teacher chose to leave out the cultural and pragmatic connotations of the phrase.

That week, James encountered some problems with the plumbing in his flat. He approached the caretaker of the building and had the following conversation in basic Arabic.

 What do you think was happening in this conversation? How do you think both parties perceived each other?

James: *Excuse me, my plumbing is broken. Can you fix it?*
Caretaker: *Yes, I will come fix it. Inshallah.*
James: *Will you come tomorrow? I really need this.*
Caretaker: *Yes, I will come tomorrow. Inshallah.*
James: *You definitely must come. What time will you come?*
Caretaker: *In the morning. Inshallah.*
James: *Yes, what time?*
Caretaker: *Morning. Inshallah.*

James was keen to pin down a time that the caretaker would come and understood *Inshallah* to mean that the caretaker was not making any promises about whether the plumbing would be fixed. James was annoyed that the caretaker hadn't asked for more details about the plumbing problem and found it inconsiderate that he had not made a more concrete plan. James wanted to push for a more definite answer than the one that the caretaker was willing to give.

The caretaker, on the other hand, perceived James as being pushy and inflexible. After all, everyone knows that we can't predict the future and so nothing is truly 100% certain. We can only deal with the problem when we come to it. The caretaker wondered if he might have misunderstood James's tone due to his low level Arabic.

After several years of living in Egypt and countless interactions with the locals, James reflected on this initial conversation and realised that his lack of cultural understanding of the phrase 'Inshallah' had led him to misjudge the intentions of his caretaker. James also realised that the Egyptians he came into contact with were much more tolerant of ambiguity than he was. He became aware of how uncomfortable he felt with uncertainty and the unknown, and sought to push for concrete plans and schedules to ease the insecurity that he felt. When deliberating Hofstede's Uncertainty Avoidance Scale (see → 'Cultural frameworks and dimensions' on page 33), James placed himself on the far end of high uncertainty avoidance.

James moved back to New Zealand after his stint in Egypt, and one day was asked to present to a group of German clients. Here is what James said after the course.

 Read what James said and consider how he might change the way he sees himself on the scale of uncertainty avoidance.

'I was giving them a presentation on the newest technology tool we'd developed, but it felt like they wanted to know everything immediately. When I was introducing the product, they wanted to know every single fact and figure associated with it. When I quoted research, they wanted to know who conducted the research and what the parameters were. When I showed them examples of what the new tool could do, they wanted to know exactly how they could do those things themselves on the spot. They wanted to be taken step by step through the application of every function of this new tool. Not only that, but when I showed them our sales projections, they wanted to know exactly how I arrived at those figures. I understand the need to be thorough, but I was exhausted by the end of the day.'

When considering his experiences in Egypt, James thought of himself as having high uncertainty avoidance and felt justified as he saw it as a methodical, structured and efficient way to be. Confronted by this group of German clients, James felt as if the tables had been turned, and he was now able to gain a different perspective of the uncertainty avoidance scale. Compared to James, these clients had a much higher level of uncertainty avoidance, and to James they felt demanding with an extreme attention to detail and a need to know and understand everything.

As James reflected on the impression his clients made on him and how they made him feel, he realised that he probably had the same effect on his Egyptian counterparts. For the first time, he saw the justifications for tolerating ambiguity and related to their 'what-will-be-will-be' approach. Having previously seen himself as high on the uncertainty avoidance scale, he was also able to empathise with the German clients and understand their need for more information and certainty. In experiencing cultures from both ends of the uncertainty avoidance scale, James was better able to put himself in the shoes of his conversation partner and understand the reasons for their behaviour. He was therefore better able to adapt to the different levels of uncertainty avoidance in his future encounters.

The level of uncertainty we can be comfortable with and the amount of detail we need in order to feel assured can differ largely from culture to culture. When faced with a level of uncertainty that we are not used to, we can sometimes assume that the other person is not communicating clearly enough. When pushed for more details than expected, we might sometimes assume the other person is being fussy or difficult. Both cases can lead to stress and miscommunication, but the ability to reflect on your experiences, as James had done, could shape the way we interact with people who have a different level of uncertainty avoidance than ourselves, thereby enabling us to focus on their intended message.

Improving understanding

Whether it is due to our diverse personalities, cultural backgrounds, or first languages, differences in our norms and expectations can lead to misunderstandings and miscommunication. This can result in a waste of time and resources and can damage relationships.

In order to avoid miscommunication, it is important that we learn to spot it when it happens and seek to clarify what might potentially be the root of any misunderstanding. The task below will help you develop your skills of misunderstanding detection.

Look at the dialogues below.
What misunderstandings could potentially arise?

1. **Marta:** *The office equipment is completely outdated. It's time we replace the technology we have and upgrade!*

   Luca: *Yes, boss. Replace the technology and upgrade. I'll get that done.*

2. **Yolanda:** *Can you send me the updated report?*

   Marie: *I'll get it done soon.*

3. **Raj:** *The contract needs to get there by tomorrow afternoon. Are you passing the post office on your way home?*

   Somchai: *No. Not really.*

4. **Seng:** *When will the project be completed?*

   Alex: *In the summer.*

5. **Jen:** *The department head just rejected my proposal without reading it properly! You're my line manager, you should have a say too!*

   Dasha: *I think your proposal is very viable. I can see you're really upset about this. I suggest you take yourself in your own hands.*

6. **Kieran:** *Did you know he came into the client meeting completely pissed? This needs to be brought to the attention of his line manager.*

   Allyson: *I know it's a bit unprofessional being pissed in front of the clients but don't you think reporting it to his manager is a bit extreme?*

7. **Mel:** *When is the AGM scheduled for?*

   Mira: *Next Wednesday.*

8. **Ana:** *I'm afraid those figures are last year's and not applicable to this year.*

   Ana's manager: *Yeah, we need to sort out the inaccuracies in the report. We need to rewrite this report before the board meeting.*

9. **Susana:** *The customer crashed into the cookie display.*

   Store Manager: *Just hoover it up.*

10. **Elizabeth:** *I thought I specifically asked you to redesign the board before I left. You didn't do it?*

    Tanya: *No.*

Philosopher Karl Popper once said, 'Always remember that it is impossible to speak in such a way that you cannot be misunderstood'. Sometimes what we intend to mean is not what is understood. Did you spot any possibilities for misunderstanding in the above dialogues? Here are some suggestions:

1   It is unclear if Marta is merely expressing her frustration or if she's asking Luca to do something about the situation. Marta's desire to 'replace the technology and upgrade' is also vague. There is the danger that without clarity about the budget and the actual specs Marta has in mind, Luca might have overestimated his understanding of what Marta wants.

2   Yolanda has not stated when she would like the report and although Marie reassures her that it will be done 'soon', it is unclear what 'soon' means to both of them.

3   Raj has made an indirect request for Somchai to go to the post office on his way home but Somchai has not picked up on this request and has simply interpreted Raj's question as Raj simply seeking information about his journey home.

4   Alex assumes that his 'summer' is the same as Seng's. It is possible that Seng is from a country in the other hemisphere or a country near the equator where summer doesn't exist.

5   In Russian and some Slovak languages, the idiomatic expression 'to take yourself in your own hands' means to regain your composure and get over the issue, not unlike the English idiom 'to pull yourself together'. Unfortunately for Dasha, the idiom resembles the English 'to take matters into your own hands'. It is possible that Jen has misunderstood Dasha's idiom and taken her comment as a suggestion that she ignores the department head and goes ahead with her proposal.

6   British English user Kieran takes the colloquialism 'pissed' to mean 'drunk' while Allyson, who is used to American English, understands 'pissed' to mean 'angry'. Also, the use of such an informal colloquialism might potentially be inappropriate in the workplace and this might make Kieran come across as unprofessional, or even unrefined.

7   Assuming that it is now Monday, for some people 'next Wednesday' could mean 'the Wednesday coming in two days' time' and for others it could mean 'the Wednesday of next week'. It is best to use actual dates to clarify which Wednesday Mira is referring to. There is also the possibility that the acronym 'AGM' does not mean the same thing to Mel and Mira.

8   Ana's manager uses 'we need to rewrite this report' to mean '*you* need to rewrite this report'. However, this might be unclear to Ana, who might leave thinking that her manager will be writing the report together with her.

9   Originating from the popular brand of vacuum cleaner 'Hoover', the verb 'to hoover' is typically used by the British to mean 'to vacuum'. However, this might not be internationally understood. Try to spot the cultural references in your speech and avoid them if they are likely to cause problems in international communication.

10   Tanya's 'no' comes without explanation and might seem abrupt and socially inappropriate to some. It is also possible that there is another interpretation of Tanya's response to Elizabeth's negative statement. Tanya's negation could mean one of two things: 'No, I didn't redesign the board,' or 'No, you're wrong. I did redesign the board'. In some languages, a 'No' response to a negative question or statement simply means 'No, I disagree with you'.

Look at the dialogues again. How can the speakers be clearer? How can they go about avoiding misunderstanding and miscommunication?

SCORE Communication Principles

Intercultural expert Kate Berardo suggests the SCORE model[29] as a set of guidelines to help us communicate effectively across cultures.

SCORE Communication Principles

Simplify and Specify	Avoid complex sentences; keep it simple; be careful with cultural references; clarify time and dates; specify what acronyms and idioms mean.
Clarify and Confirm	Clarify what you are saying; check that you understand what the other person is saying; ask for clarification whenever necessary.
Organise and Outline	Ensure a clear structure; number your main points; in written communication, make use of bullet points, clear headings and subject lines.
Rephrase and Reframe	Use different words to say the same thing; use synonyms and paraphrase; use metaphors, if necessary, to help the other person understand.
Explain with examples	Explain what you mean; give reasons and help the other person see why; provide examples to clarify.

Reprinted from *Building Cultural Competence: Innovative Activities and Models* edited by Kate Berardo and Darla K. Deardorff (Sterling, VA: Stylus Publishing, LLC) with permission of the publisher, Copyright © 2012, Stylus Publishing, LLC.

While Berardo does not suggest that we apply all the principles of SCORE in every conversation we have, the model is particularly useful when communicating an important point, explaining a complex process or simply when you detect a potential for misunderstanding. We can selectively use the above guidelines and adapt them to the situations and the conversation partners we encounter. An attempt to over-clarify might come across as condescending to some, and therefore it is sometimes useful to gently add a version of the following disclaimer, '*I'm sorry if I'm repeating this/asking about this again but you know, sometimes in international communication, miscommunication can happen. This is important to me and so I just want to be sure to avoid any possible misunderstandings.*'

---

29 In Berardo K & Deardorff DK (2012) *Building Cultural Competence*. pp225–230. Sterling, VA, USA: Stylus Publishing.

Being aware of miscommunication

Listen to the interactions that take place around you. How many possible instances of miscommunication do you hear? How are the speakers around you applying elements of the SCORE model?

Be aware of the interactions you have. Which elements of the SCORE model can you use to help facilitate effective communication?

To put it simply, communication is the coding and decoding of messages. As a listener, we tend to decode the messages we receive using our own framework and understanding of the world. As a speaker, we tend to code messages in a way that we ourselves would understand – something that would work well if we were communicating with people identical to ourselves.

An increased awareness and understanding of how others different to ourselves might code and decode messages could help us ensure that we get the right message, and that we get the right messages across. Perhaps then we might learn to decode messages using the other's framework and code messages in a way they will understand.

Chapter 6: Listening actively

How we listen

When I first met my accountant, Mary, I was dreading a meeting that I thought would be filled with technical jargon and complex conversations about finance that would only confuse and overwhelm me. When I was seated comfortably in her office, she started asking me questions about how I'd like her to help me. As I spoke, she listened attentively. Aside from the occasional note she would make in her notepad, Mary would look at me with interested eyes, as if she was taking in every bit of information I was giving her, no matter how trivial.

Whenever I made certain statements based on my limited financial and legal knowledge, or whenever I voiced my assumptions on how things worked, I half-expected her to interrupt me with a correction or a clarification to stop me from going in the wrong direction with my thought process.

However, Mary never interrupted me. She would listen, no matter how ridiculous my assumptions or financial ignorance might be. She would allow me to finish voicing each of my thoughts, conscious that I was sometimes thinking aloud as I spoke. Not once did she make me feel like she was being impatient with me or silently judging me. And when she did speak, I was ready to listen to her and to benefit from her expertise for I felt that she now had a clear picture of my circumstances and understood how best to help me. Throughout our meeting, she created an atmosphere of calm and ease where time stopped in that room just for me.

I came out of that room thinking much more clearly about my finances, armed with new knowledge and fresh ideas as to how to proceed. I felt refreshed by our interaction and committed to the new relationship we had just embarked on. I started to think about some of the people I had come into contact with in my past who could have benefitted from Mary's listening skills: customer service personnel who are so keen to jump in to defend themselves rather than hear me out, caring friends and family who good-naturedly come in with advice after advice before understanding how I would like to be helped, managers in a rush to ensure everyone gets to the point quickly and not waste any time.

Despite its multiple benefits, the essential communication skill of listening actively is not always present in our daily interactions, which was probably why my encounter with Mary made such an impression. I myself have been guilty of only remembering half of what I have heard because my mind was too busy trying to multi-task. So, what does it mean to listen actively?

Improving listening skills

Below are ten tips for improving our listening skills.

❶ Listen. Really listen.

Sometimes we think we are listening but we do so only until we hear something that we have an opinion on or something that triggers our memory of an anecdote that we'd like to tell. Our mind then starts to prepare our responses and we wait for our turn to speak, paying attention to cues that might indicate that our conversation partner has finished their turn. Somewhere along the line, we have stopped really listening to what is being said. We might think we look like we are listening but we are no longer processing the information that the speaker is conveying.

Instead, resist the impulse to react. Focus on understanding the speaker, rather than on responding to the speaker. As communications trainer and author Bob Dignen suggests, try staying in the other person's world a little longer.

❷ Respect the speaker.

The speaker has a right to speak and so respect their right to express their opinions or points of view. Avoid displaying your disagreement or any negativity with your expressions or body language before giving your conversation partner the chance to fully express what they need to say. Instead, let them talk and consider the reasons behind why they might be saying what they are saying. Respect also includes giving them your full attention, so try to avoid multi-tasking e.g. checking your mobile phone, looking for someone else to speak to, doodling or fidgeting when they are speaking.

❸ Show that you are listening.

Nothing can be more discouraging than speaking to someone who clearly isn't paying attention to what you're saying, or someone who might be listening but isn't sending you the right signals to let you know that they are.

You might claim that you are able to listen while playing Solitaire on your laptop or scrolling through your social media feeds, and this might be true, but this could distract the speaker from their thought processes and their ability to articulate themselves.

Consider what you can do to show actively that you think what the speaker is saying is valuable and that you are listening. This might include looking interested, maintaining eye contact, nodding and smiling or using appropriate facial expressions. Your body language can also say a lot about your interest in what is being said. A closed posture with folded arms and a body tilted away from the speaker could be seen as defensive or disinterested. By facing the speaker and adopting an open posture, you could come across as accessible and friendly. (However, see ➔'Cultural considerations' on page 107 for more on cultural differences with regards to these signals.) You could also show your interest by making encouraging sounds like 'Hmm … mmm' and 'Huh huh', making short comments about what is said e.g. 'Really?'; 'I didn't know that!' or nodding your head.

❹ Hold back judgments & don't interrupt.

The second step of the ADAPT model (see ➔chapter 2, page 45) involves not judging and remaining open-minded, but our internal voice sometimes makes judgments so instinctively that it can be hard to stop ourselves. While someone is talking, we often seek to make sense of what is being said by considering how we relate to it. We formulate our opinion, and we are keen to let them know what we think and how we feel. So we interrupt.

However, by forcing ourselves to hold back and allow the speaker to finish, we can train ourselves to avoid selective listening and premature evaluations. Author of bestseller *Time to Think*[30], Nancy Kline, suggests that when we truly listen we create an environment that allows the speaker to think for themselves and to find creative solutions to their problems. And one of the ways we can create such a conducive thinking space is by helping the speaker realise that you are listening attentively and that you are not going to interrupt them. (However, see ➔'Cultural considerations' on page 107 for cultural differences in turn taking.)

---

30 Kline N (1999) *Time to Think*. London: Ward Lock.

❺ Be curious. Ask questions.

A conversation is not simply a space for you to make announcements and voice your own opinions. It is a space for two or more people to share information, communicate their thoughts and feelings, work out plans and solutions, brainstorm ideas and negotiate meaning. Once we understand that, we can start to appreciate how much we can learn a lot from our interactions. By cultivating our sense of curiosity about others, we no longer listen out of sheer politeness but out of a sincere desire to find out about the other person's experiences, ideas, thoughts and viewpoints. The questions we ask then go beyond display questions to show our interest and stem from us genuinely wanting to know more and wanting to connect.

The questions we ask can not only shape the way a conversation goes but can also frame the relationship that we are developing with the speaker. Very often, when someone brings up a problem, an annoyance, or a challenge they are facing, our instinct is to put on our advisors' hat and start offering advice and suggesting solutions that we think might help the speaker. Sometimes, we disguise our advice in directive questions such as, *'Would it not be better speak to your manager about this?'* or, *'Why don't you just ignore him?'* when in actual fact the speaker might be seeking a listening ear and not advice. After all, unsolicited advice given without a complete understanding of the situation and the background can sometimes be frustrating.

However, if we consider the way a coach uses questions to bring out the best in their clients, we could become attuned to a way of asking questions in a non-directive way that would instead allow the speaker to develop their thoughts and ideas freely. Questions like, *'What do you think is the best thing to do now?'* or, *'What might be the consequences of making that decision?'* can give the speaker the space to explore the issues and discover the answers within themselves. By asking the right questions we could support the speaker to find optimal solutions to their challenges without being prescriptive.

❻ Use their name.

Our names are a symbol of our identity and help distinguish us from the crowd. When someone addresses us using our name, we feel recognised and validated as individuals. People who use the names of the people they are addressing are often seen as better listeners who are engaged in an interaction rather than simply using the conversation as a platform for self-promotion. However, avoid over doing this because it can come across as over-enthusiastic or even patronising. Nevertheless, appropriate use of your conversation partner's name can be an occasional reminder that you value them as an individual. Also, do be aware of how the speaker prefers to be addressed e.g. should you use their surname or first name? Should you be using their title?

❼ Try to feel what the speaker is feeling.

When someone is describing a harrowing experience, an annoying encounter or an exciting prospect, try to put yourself in their shoes and try to feel what they are feeling. This will enable you to better understand the impact that the described situation has on the speaker, and help you connect you with them. Such a demonstration of empathy and understanding can also help the speaker feel truly listened to, and therefore put them at greater ease in their conversation with you.

❽ Clarify and summarise what is being said.

If the speaker is giving important information such as reports on progress, task instructions, conditions of a negotiation etc, make use of clarification strategies to ensure that you have understood them correctly. Clarify any unknown terms, acronyms and vague language. If a concept is confusing or potentially misleading, summarise what is being said. By starting with phrases like, *'So what you're saying is ...'*; *'Do you mean to say ...?'*; *'If I understood you correctly, you're saying that ...'*, you are allowing them the chance to clarify. The act of summarising also allows you to process and articulate this information, thus making it more memorable.

If the speaker is simply sharing a problem with you, the process of clarification could help the speaker see the issue from a slightly different angle and allow them to gain a new perspective. It will also help you make an impression as an active listener.

❾ Respond appropriately.

Be open and honest with your responses but be careful with negativity. You might want to disagree with the speaker but there is little value you can add to the interaction by attacking them or putting them down. You also do not want to look like you've been waiting for your turn to speak so that you could launch into a series of attacks. Show that you've been listening and carefully considering what is being said.

Rather than making declarative absolute statements, be measured and clear when you're talking about your own perceptions or feelings, using sentence starters like, *'It seems to me that ...'*, *'I feel that ...'*, *'What you are saying leads me to think that...'*. Listen with respect and respond with respect too.

⑩ Don't assume you know what the speaker wants from the interaction.

When someone shares a problem with us, we often think that they are coming to us for advice. We rush in with our solutions not realising that perhaps all they wanted was to rant and for us to lend a listening ear. Interruptions often happen because we assume we know what the speaker wants to say, and that we are saving time by jumping in.

Consider the scenario below.

What assumptions is the shop assistant making? How might the conversation play out if she hadn't interrupted?

Harry approaches a shop assistant in a department store...

Harry: *Excuse me, could you tell me where the shoe department is?*

Shop Assistant: *The shoe department is on the third floor. Right behind the men's shirts.*

Harry: *I was told it's on this floor because I'm ...*

Shop Assistant: *No, it's not on this floor. Shoe department's on the third floor. Right behind the men's shirts.*

Harry: *But I asked the lady downstairs for ...*

Shop Assistant: *Take this escalator up to the third floor and you'll find it. Men's shoes. Right behind men's shirts.*

Harry: *Sorry, I don't think it's ...*

Shop Assistant: *That's the only men's shoes department in this building. You're not going to find men's shoes on this floor.*

Harry: *I'm not looking for the men's shoes department. I'm looking for the toilets. I was told they are behind the ladies' shoes department.*

💬 The shop assistant has had to respond to multiple customers asking for directions through her working day and might have started making assumptions about the customer's needs in order to be more efficient. When she saw Harry asking for the whereabouts of the shoe department, she immediately assumed that because he was male he would be looking for the men's shoes department. However, by constantly interrupting Harry and not letting him finish, she did not realise that he was in fact looking for the toilets behind the women's shoes department until much later in the conversation. Her attempt to be efficient ended up taking both of them more time and probably left Harry feeling frustrated.

The above scenario might not be unfamiliar to us. We have all encountered situations where we have been interrupted due to misinterpretations of our intentions or assumptions about what we are about to say. Situations like this often end with the speakers feeling annoyed and sometimes choosing to give up on their attempt to communicate rather than being misunderstood repeatedly. No matter how much we think we know, we probably know less about what the speakers are going to say than the speakers themselves. So don't be in a rush to complete the sentence for someone else and allow them space and time think and articulate their thoughts.

Cultural considerations

When I first started presenting at conferences, it was common practice to have members of the audience taking notes on their notepads and looking intently at the presenter to show that they were listening. As technology evolved, I started seeing more and more smart phones in the audience, and members of the audience would tap away on their phones during a presentation. I've seen some presenters get quite annoyed. Their assumption was that these audience members were being disrespectful, replying to emails, playing games or checking social media updates on their phones instead of paying attention to the presentation.

It then became known that some members of the audience were actually using their phones to make notes or write live social media posts of the presentation they were attending, therefore extending the reach of the presenter and serving to publicise the event to people who were unable to attend the conference. When presenters came to realise this, they became a lot more accepting and even welcoming of the use of phones, treating it as a sign that people were listening to their presentation.

Like in the example above, our perceptions of what constitutes active listening can sometimes depend on our norms and expectations, which in turn can be influenced by our culture (industry, corporate, national or otherwise). Moreover, our norms might not be the norms of others, and these norms can change with time, and an attitude of openness and flexibility can help us deal with different ways of listening.

Below are some features of active listening that might be interpreted differently depending on the expected norms.

 Look at the critical incidents below. What do you think is happening in each of the scenarios?

1. Company CFO Hugh was talking to one of his accounts executives, Naomi, who kept looking down at the floor when he was speaking. Hugh wondered if Naomi had done something wrong and was not able to look him in the eye.

2. Sienna became quite disconcerted by a client who seemed to like listening with his eyes closed. Whenever Sienna launched into any kind of description or explanation, this client would close his eyes. Sienna wondered if the client was so bored talking to her that he was napping during their conversations.

3. Andreas was in an important meeting with Ken and was keen for it to go well. To show that he was listening, whenever Ken spoke, Andreas would put on a serious face and lean forward. In contrast with Andreas's upright posture, Ken had one arm around the back of his chair that seemed to support his body weight as he relaxed into it. Ken wanted to reassure Andreas that the topics they were addressing in that meeting did not stress him and that he was in a relaxed state, ready to deal with the issues. However, the two men came out of the meeting feeling uneasy.

4. Kimberly and Anna were put on the same project team and were meeting on a video call for the first time. Kimberly greeted Anna with a big smile and smiled while listening to Anna to try and put her at ease. Anna, however, looked stern and did not crack a smile during their entire video conversation, and this left Kimberly feeling upset. Later, Kimberly was heard using words like 'unfriendly', 'disapproving', 'solemn', 'miserable' and 'gloomy' to describe Anna.

5. Kelly got one of her first jobs in Venezuela where she ended up living and working for nine years. At first she found it hard adapting to the way people tended to interrupt each other in group conversations, but she soon got used to it. Kelly was offered a new job in Switzerland, which she accepted. However, when she moved there she felt great difficulty talking to her group of Swiss colleagues. She didn't think they were great conversationalists because when she spoke they would look at her solemnly in silence. As they seemed to have nothing to say, Kelly would resume speaking in the hope of relieving the uncomfortable silence.

 Were you able to identify the features that caused an issue in the interactions?

1 Eye contact (Hugh and Naomi)

To some, maintaining eye contact with the speaker demonstrates that the listener is listening with full attention, and the inability to look at someone in the eye implies guilt and wrongdoing. To others, maintaining eye contact with the opposite sex might convey flirtatious feelings. In some hierarchical societies, making eye contact may be considered rude, especially when listening to a teacher, a senior manager or anyone who is in authority over you. Whether the norm is to look at the speaker's nose or to stare straight ahead or at the floor when being spoken to, we can easily find out what cultural expectations might be by observing other members of the same community before adjusting our expectations and adapting our behaviour, if necessary. (See → Chapter 10 for more on eye contact.)

2 Closing your eyes (Sienna and the client)

To someone who is used to eye contact from their listeners, this practice could be interpreted as sleepiness, boredom or even a disrespectful way of blocking the speaker out. Sienna eventually had a non-confrontational talk about this with the client and found out that her client liked closing his eyes so as to better concentrate on what was being said. The open conversation made them more aware of each other's norms and assumptions, which helped them become more mindful of each other's expectations and more flexible with their own.

3 Body language (Andreas and Ken)

Some might use body language to indicate how respectfully and attentively they are listening. However, the interpretation of this non-verbal behaviour is not always universal. In this case, Andreas thought that Ken wasn't taking him seriously at all and found his behaviour disrespectful. He felt that Ken believed in his own superiority over Andreas and was not interested in listening to anything Andreas had to say. Ken, meanwhile, thought that Andreas was uptight and controlling and felt that Andreas started to get confrontational and aggressive when he leant in.

Both men were making multiple assumptions based on their own norms and expectations. In international communication, it is important to be aware of the assumptions that we make and to consider other possible interpretations rather than jumping to conclusions.

4 Smiles (Kimberly and Anna)

Smiling is very much related to the culture we are used to and is a way of communicating certain messages to others. In some cultures, a smile says, 'I'm listening to you' or, 'I'm friendly', 'I'm sincere' or, 'I'm open for a chat'. But in others it says, 'you're a close friend' or, 'I've just had something really amazing happen to me' or even, 'I'm trying to hide a negative feeling'.

While Kimberly might have found an un-smiling Anna unapproachable and difficult to talk to, Anna might have felt that Kimberly's constant smiles were insincere, condescending or even creepy. She might also end up thinking of Kimberly as a frivolous character who wasn't serious about the project or her job. Be aware that not everyone smiles when listening, and that a smile might not necessarily mean what you think it means. (See ➔ Chapter 10 for more on smiling.)

5 Turn-taking (Kelly and her Venezuelan and Swiss colleagues)

Turn-taking is a fascinating skill that involves listening and knowing when to start and finish your turn in a conversation. This means looking for cues that the speaker has finished speaking, clues that might come in the form of language, the pitch and volume of the voice, the eye movement of the speaker or body language, etc. Despite the complexity of such a skill, most of us pick it up in infanthood, during conversations with our parents. As such, the way we take turns can be so ingrained in us that minute differences in turn-taking habits can serve to make us feel uncomfortable.

Some writers[1] have used the concept of sport to categorise the three main turn-taking styles of group conversations, dividing them into 'Rugby', 'Bowling' and 'Basketball'. Like the game of rugby, Rugby turn-takers are usually comfortable with quick-pace, regular interruptions and overlapping of speech, shorter turns with quick changes of speakers, and conversations that tend to take place at a louder volume.

Bowling turn-takers, on the other hand, tend to be used to a slower pace, a lower volume, and longer pauses between turns, to allow time for listeners to process what they have heard. Interruptions might be seen as inappropriate or rude. Basketball turn-takers seem to fall in between Rugby and Bowling turn-takers. There might be short pauses in between turns but pauses can also be a chance for another speaker to steal the floor. Basketball turn-takers therefore use a variety of strategies to ensure that listeners know that they are not done with their turn yet.

In the critical incident above, Kelly may have come from a Basketball culture but moved to a community with a Rugby style of turn-taking. Having got used to the level of interruptions and the lack of long pauses in group conversations, Kelly interpreted her new colleagues' silences to mean that they had nothing to say or that they were not interested in a conversation. She then started to fill what she thought of as the awkward silence with her own voice.

Being used to a bowling style of turn-taking, Kelly's new colleagues might have found her incessant chat tiring and wondered why she doesn't give others a chance to have a turn. Interestingly, there might be only milliseconds of a difference between the pauses in a Rugby culture and a Bowling culture, but these milliseconds can lead to a world of misinterpretations and misunderstandings.

There could be a tendency to attribute the Bowling culture to countries like Switzerland, Korea, Japan and Taiwan; the Rugby culture to countries like Venezuela, Spain, Brazil and Italy; and the Basketball culture to countries like the UK, the USA and Australia. However, we must also remember that turn-taking habits can also differ from region to region (within a country), industry to industry, family to family, and person to person. It is therefore important that we avoid assuming that someone is rude or disinterested simply based on the level of interruptions and pauses they are comfortable or not comfortable with.

---

1   Steinbach S (1996) *Fluent American English*. Davis, CA: The Seabright Group

The importance of being an active listener

Many people claim to be good listeners, but being a truly active listener can enable you to improve communication channels, enhance relationships, remember what has been said, better understand the situations and issues faced, promote commitment to you and your team, and allow your conversation partner to grow and develop. However, listening and interpreting are two different stages and it is vital to remember that how we interpret things might not be the way they were meant.

'Effective listeners remember that "words have no meaning – people have meaning". The assignment of meaning to a term is an internal process; meaning comes from inside us. And although our experiences, knowledge and attitudes differ, we often misinterpret each other's messages while under the illusion that a common understanding has been achieved.'[31]

---

31 Barker L & K Watson (2000) *Listen Up: How to improve relationships, reduce stress and be more productive by using the power of listening.* New York: St. Martin's Press.

Chapter 7: Leadership communication

Managing and being managed

What is the role of a manager?
We start this chapter by looking at our different expectations of managers and what we think they should be there to do; but before I tell you the story of the manager Natalia (using the task below), take a moment to consider what your beliefs and attitudes might be towards the role of a manager.

 Imagine if you were put in a new project team with a manager you have never met. Look at the list below and tick five that you find most important.

The manager is there so as:

- To control what happens in the team.
- To instruct the team on what to do.
- To co-ordinate and organise the team.
- To give general guidance to the team.
- To help and counsel when problems occur.
- To encourage input from the team.
- To motivate the team.
- To develop the strengths of the individuals on the team.
- To improve team performance.
- To set an example for the team by doing it themselves.
- To cultivate good relationships within the team.
- To mediate among team members and manage conflicts.

Now consider the case below.

Which of the above expectations did Natalia have of her role as manager?

Which of the above expectations did her Swedish team members have?

What can happen when these expectations don't match?

Natalia worked for a multinational firm, heading one of the top sales teams in Sao Paulo, Brazil. She was an employee with a lot of potential and offered the opportunity to move up the organisational ladder by taking a transfer to head a team in Sweden. Natalia welcomed the opportunity to show the headquarters her leadership skills: to take charge and lead her team to success. However, not long into her new role she started to face issues with her new team members.

Although they seemed friendly, she didn't feel like they respected her as a leader or trusted her expertise. They were constantly knocking on her door to question her decisions or to suggest a different way of doing things, and even when she'd given them specific instructions to carry out a task, they would often do it their own way without checking with her. She found team meetings most difficult to handle: her team members would disagree with her or challenge what she'd said in front of the rest of the team, which she sometimes thought was humiliating. Even when she had explicitly said that she had made a decision on something, they would act as if it was still up for discussion, giving their own opinions on how they should change or adjust things.

After weeks of frustration, Natalia emailed her line manager in the Stockholm head office about the issues she was facing with her team. Her manager replied with a couple of questions, asking her if she felt her team was still performing and achieving the targets, and what she thought would help her better collaborate with her team members. Natalia felt that her line manager was being vague and was extremely dissatisfied with this outcome.

Having reached the end of her tether, Natalia decided to get advice from a communications trainer who encouraged her to consider getting feedback on her leadership style from her team members. Initially, she found this a difficult step to make as she wasn't used to the concept of managers asking their subordinates for feedback, but using the ADAPT model (see ➝ Chapter 2, page 45), she persuaded herself that having an open conversation with her team about her leadership was in line with her own beliefs in the merits of getting to know her team members, building a better relationship and forming stronger bonds with them.

Natalia's team members were pleased to be asked for their thoughts on her leadership and openly expressed that they were not used to being told what to do. They had found her tasks and instructions over-specific, leaving them no room for initiative and creative freedom. Her tendency to control and take charge was creating resentment among the team and they felt that she didn't trust them to do their job well. They could see that she wasn't happy when they tried to challenge or make changes to her decisions, and found this surprising because that's how they've always worked.

In her years as a top manager in Brazil, Natalia had become used to one management style that worked for her and her team in Sao Paulo. She came to realise that when she tried to transpose her style onto her new team in Sweden, problems arose and she was left feeling frustrated and confused. While her team in Brazil might have been comfortable with a more directive style that involved their manager being the one with the expertise taking control and giving them specific instructions, her team in Sweden expected a flatter hierarchy where decision-making was more decentralised and democratic, and where the manager acted as a motivator and a coach.

Management styles

When we discuss management styles, we are often talking about the way managers organise their teams and ensure that their objectives are achieved. This also includes the way managers treat their subordinates and team members, and the relationships they have with them. Different management styles have been described and grouped in a variety of ways by different writers.

In the late 1950s and 60s, Douglas McGregor described the two broad categories: Theory X (which described a more autocratic and directive management style) and Theory Y (which described a more consultative and participative management style) that served to address the level of authority that a manager asserts on their team[32].

---

32 McGregor DM (1957) "The Human Side of Enterprise". In: *Adventure in Thought and Action*. Proceedings of the Fifth Anniversary Convocation of the School of Industrial Management, Massachusetts Institute of Technology. Cambridge, MA: MIT.

Over the years, models outlining six or seven categories of management styles were developed[33], all endeavouring to describe the different ways decisions are made, the different focuses that managers have, the different levels of control/guidance employed, and the different roles that they take on. The area of cross-cultural studies offers further descriptions[34] of the typical management styles we can expect from different countries.

These models have been very useful in developing our understanding of the range of possible ways to manage a team, and also in encouraging us to become aware of our own default management style and helping us reflect on what the most effective way might be for our circumstances. After all, there are pros and cons to each style and there is no one-size-fits-all approach. A manager who is flexible and willing to adapt would utilise a style that suits the team members, the situation and the corporate culture. And when managers enter a different work environment e.g. when they have to work with a different culture, it becomes vital that they are sensitive towards the different management styles that their team members might be used to, and are able to develop a style that can work for all who are involved.

Coming from a high power distance culture – where groups tend to be more hierarchical and authority figures are expected to have more power (see ➜ 'Cultural frameworks and dimensions' on page 33) – Natalia was used to a more directive/authoritative management style and her team in Sao Paulo appreciated the detailed guidance and clear direction that she was able to provide through her leadership. However, moving to a lower power distance culture where there is more equality and authority is regularly challenged, Natalia's style was not a good match for her team. Although it is not too late for Natalia to make adjustments to the way she manages her team, it would have made a big difference to her integration if she had spent some time during her initial move trying to gain a better understanding of the management culture of her new working environment.

The dangers of over-applying management styles or cultural frameworks

While the concept of high and low power distance can be useful in explaining the way a group of people might regard authority, we must be careful not to assume that all high power distance cultures will favour a management style similar to Natalia's.

---

33 For example, see https://www.breathehr.com/blog/best-management-styles-and-how-to-use-them (accessed November 2018).

34 For example: Lewis R (1996) *When Cultures Collide: Leading across cultures.* Nicholas Brealey Publishing.

❶ Consider the critical incident below. What do you think was happening?

Irish global bank manager Andy was given the task of leading a Japanese team to manage a product re-launch in Japan. Knowing that he was dealing with a high power distance culture, Andy assumed that they would turn to him for all decision-making and detailed delegation of responsibilities. He felt his beliefs were further confirmed when his team members remained silent in all their team meetings, despite his repeated invitation for them to contribute their ideas. Taking on a more directive style, Andy began making decisions and delegating without any consultation with his team. This did not go down well with his team and one day one of his team members told him that his team was not too happy with the way he was taking decisions into his own hands.

💬 Although Andy's team respected his authority, consensus among team members was of great importance to them.

Issues are usually discussed and decisions are not usually made until all the members have had a chance to voice their thoughts. These discussions, however, may not take place in a team meeting where Andy is present, as the team members preferred to not openly disagree with their manager for fear of causing him to lose face (see ➝ 'Dealing with intercultural communication' on page 75 for more on Face). Instead, team members were used to having pre-meeting discussions that could take place in the form of email communication or a meeting without their manager. When a consensus is reached, this would then be communicated and ratified in the official team meeting with their manager.

Andy's misunderstanding of his team's expectations might have been based on his willingness to adapt to a different way of doing things, but such assumptions can also lead to ineffective leadership. It could be risky over-generalising what the preferred management styles might be, especially when there can be much variation due to corporate culture, education background, social status etc. Furthermore, as more and more multinational conglomerates build their organisations across borders, the way teams are managed is becoming influenced by the dominant culture of their parent company.

Understanding the management culture of your new environment

So, how could Andy and Natalia gain a better understanding of their new teams and their new working environment?

 ## Working environments

Below is a list of questions to ask when observing a new work environment that we are coming into.

Decision making

● Who usually makes the decisions?
  ● the manager
  ● the manager together with the employees
  ● the employees

● Who is consulted before decisions are made?
● How are they consulted? E.g. In a meeting? Via emails?
● Is a consensus needed for a decision to be made? If so, how is that consensus usually reached?
● Are decisions reversible/changeable?

Relationships across hierarchies

● Are there many levels of hierarchy in the organisation?
● Can team members drop in to discuss things with the manager at any time?
● How visible are the managers during the day?
● Are managers expected to work alongside their staff e.g. if they want their staff working overtime, would they stay and work overtime too?
● Do managers spend time with their team members after working hours?
● Can subordinates communicate directly with upper management and top executives? For example, in an email, can one cc the manager of the recipient? Can the manager of one team write directly to the participant of another team asking for information, bypassing their team leader? How is such 'level-skipping' perceived?

Tasks

- Is the manager expected to provide clear direction for the team?
- How specific are the instructions that managers give? Is there space for improvisation and creativity?
- How involved are the mangers in day-to-day operations?

Do note that the answers to the above questions are not meant to try and fit the observed management style into any pre-existing category. The answers can exist in any permutation and combination, some of which might initially seem surprising. But they can help us better understand the culture of management of our new team/manager.

Speaking out to management

The line between confidence and arrogance is sometimes a thin one, and what might come across as having confidence in one's own abilities to some might be interpreted as being smug and self-serving to others. Not everyone finds it acceptable to challenge or disagree with their manager and not everyone would find it easy to speak of their own achievements in order to get ahead.

 Consider the critical incident below. What are the possible interpretations for Jenny's behaviour. What values and attitudes underlie her actions?

Jenny has been working in a large American petroleum company since she moved to the US from Taiwan several months ago, but she has found it difficult to speak up in the way her other colleagues seem to. There had been many projects that Jenny had been interested in working on, teams she had felt confident in leading, and responsibilities that she had been keen on undertaking, but each time her colleagues had voiced their interests and sold themselves as the perfect candidates for the job while Jenny had kept her wishes and aspirations to herself. Even during her one-to-one appraisals, Jenny found it hard talking to her managers about how her own career development. As a result, her colleagues have been taking on the new challenges and leaving her behind.

For most of her working life, Jenny had been working within a more collectivist culture (see → Chapter 2, page 35) and enjoys being a part of a team where everyone worked for success as a unit, and not to serve themselves. In her experience, promotion opportunities, leadership positions and interesting tasks often go to those who are most capable for the job, and capability is often proven by hard work and a good track record. In her world, hard work and effort does not usually go unnoticed, and those who shout the loudest about their achievements are often looked upon suspiciously by management. After all, as the saying goes, 'Empty vessels make the most noise'.

Coming into an individualist culture where self-promotion is necessary in getting noticed, Jenny found it confusing. She was disappointed that her hard work was going unnoticed, and that her humility and her reluctance to brag about her abilities was now seen as a disadvantage and not a virtue. With the help of some coaching, Jenny applied the ADAPT model (see → 'Dealing with intercultural communication' on page 43).

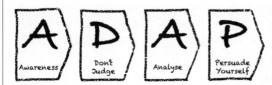

Awareness	I am feeling frustrated and disappointed. I expected the managers to see all the hard work and long hours I'm putting into the company but nobody seems to notice anything. They only notice it if you speak about what you do and the great things you have done. I find that difficult to do because I feel like that signifies arrogance, pride and selfishness.
Don't judge	I am tempted to judge my colleagues who speak up but I am aware that they are from a different culture from me and are used to different norms.
Analyse	My colleagues feel that those who cannot talk about their achievements and abilities are not confident and do not believe in themselves. Self-confidence is a positive trait that enables us to solve problems, instill positivity in the people around, and make progress. The managers seem to believe that those without confidence cannot lead or go further in their careers.

Persuade yourself	I know that I am good at my job and I know that I am ready for new opportunities. I would like my managers to know that I believe in my own abilities and perhaps I can find ways that are not arrogant or self-serving to make them notice my contribution to the company and my desire to advance my career. Things I have learnt from my past experience and my expertise can also help my team. I also realised that I find it easier to express this in writing because it feels like I am formally reporting on my progress rather than bragging about my achievements.
Try	I try to remember that my managers may not notice my work unless I remind them. When I am contributing my expertise to the team, I try to mention my previous experience and achievements in a way that does not look like I'm showing off. If there is a project or a position I am hoping to get, I will write an email expressing my wishes.

In Jenny's case, she was able to find a way that enabled her to speak up without betraying her innate values and beliefs while ensuring that she would be noticed in her new work environment. However, if you are a manager used to a more vocal team, it can be a challenge to find out the thoughts and opinions of your more deferent team members.

Consider the following critical incident and suggest ways that Astrid can get her team members to speak up.

Norwegian telecommunications expert Astrid was asked to lead a virtual team based in China to help brainstorm ideas to solve a pressing problem their department was facing. She was excited to hear from her team of experts but she quickly realised that her meetings often started with her giving a few examples in an attempt to get things going and those tended to be the only suggestions voiced. Astrid tried asking each team member to give their opinions but was often faced with either silence or a polite nod of approval towards her sample suggestions. Astrid came away from each meeting describing the experience as, *'harder than getting blood from a stone'*.

Brainstorming meetings might work well in certain cultures, but when working with a more hierarchical culture that features a high power distance (see → 'Managing and being managed' on page 113), it can be problematic as a manager trying to get the team to speak out, especially in a context where the success of the meeting largely depends on their contributions. Making suggestions that might seem to contradict their manager's ideas could cause their superior to lose face, something that could be perceived as disrespectful, even defiant. In addition, those from more collectivist cultures might find it uncomfortable when put on the spot to display one's creativity and experience in front of their colleagues. A poor suggestion or idea could potentially result in a loss of face, while a brilliant one could end up looking like an attempt to show off, thus alienating themselves from the team.

Meetings at work

So, what can managers do to encourage the participants of a meeting to have their say? Here are some suggestions:

- Allow time for participants to prepare before the meeting. Circulate the agenda, and if there is a discussion or a brainstorming session to be had, ensure that participants know what it will be about so that they can think about it in advance and prepare their opinions and ideas.

- In some cultures, participants prefer to have a meeting among themselves before the actual meeting. In this pre-meeting, participants can freely voice their thoughts and come to a consensus without the presence of their superior. The actual meeting then becomes a place to present what has been agreed for a stamp of approval from their manager.

- During the meeting, divide participants into smaller groups to discuss ideas so that the individual is not put on the spot in front of a large group. It might be more reassuring when presenting an argument or a suggestion as a group.

- If possible, allow for anonymous thoughts or ideas to be submitted. When a discussion or feedback is required, consider having an opinion/feedback box that participants could contribute to before the meeting. When on-the-spot brainstorming is necessary, get participants to write their ideas down anonymously on cards that can be collected, read out and discussed.

- Create a conducive atmosphere that encourages co-operation, acceptance, and supportive interaction. Explicitly remind participants each time that there is no such thing as a stupid idea or opinion. Every idea has the chance of developing into a better one with the help of the group.

- Appeal to the goals of the group. Remind the group of what they are there to achieve and the importance of working together to achieve those targets. Help them see that the individual's expertise and knowledge can serve the group as a whole.

While the national or regional culture might affect someone's views on speaking out, individual personality differences can also have an influence on their preferences for speaking out and spontaneous brainstorming. Some might find it easier to talk on a one-on-one basis, others might find it more gratifying to bounce ideas around in a large group. Some introverts might prefer not to be put on the spot in front of others, while some extroverts might enjoy having a platform to voice their opinions but might struggle to listen and respond sensitively to others in the room.

Whether these differences are due to culture or to personalities, one thing to remember is that there is no one-size-fits-all method for getting your team to speak out, but with some patience and awareness we should be able to hear what every person has to say.

Giving and receiving feedback

Giving and receiving feedback can be a problematic area, especially when the feedback is not entirely positive. It can sometimes be hard to stomach negative feedback, and in order to encourage the receiver to be more receptive to the developmental feedback, the Hamburger Approach, aka *the Feedback Sandwich*, has become commonplace in some cultures.

This three-layer approach is characterised by the two buns and the meat of a hamburger, with the buns representing the positive aspects of the feedback, and the meat representing the developmental feedback that the receiver needs to consider. The compliments and praise not only serve to soften the blow of the negative feedback but also acknowledge the positive things that the receiver has done, reaffirming that behaviour and encouraging them to continue developing those positive aspects.

In some cultures, however, the Hamburger Approach could be seen as merely pandering to the egos of the receiver, and a more direct method is favoured, going straight for the meat and leaving out the buns. In others, particularly cultures that prefer a high context style of communication, being too direct with negative feedback could risk a loss of face for the receiver, and it might be the norm to just deliver the buns and leave the receiver to figure out what the meat might be for themselves.

Consider the examples of feedback below and decide which feedback fits (a) the Hamburger approach, (b) the all-meat-no-buns approach, or (c) the all-buns-but-read-in-between-the-lines-for-the-meat approach.

1. 'I thought the event wasn't very well organised. The people invited did not really make up our target market and they didn't fully understand what the product was supposed to do.'

2. 'I thought you did a great job organising the event. The venue was perfect and the food was excellent. You went to a lot of effort inviting so many people, but I'm not sure if they were really our target market. I felt that they didn't fully understand what our product was supposed to do. Do you think we could target our invitations for the next launch? Having said that, the competition at the end was great. It encouraged people to get hands-on experience with the product. So well done.'

3. 'I thought you did a good job organising the event. The venue, the food, and the competition at the end was all very good. Do you think the people you invited understood our product? Because it is important that they are able to explain its features to their audience, don't you think? Anyway, well done.'

Answers: 1 b; 2 a; 3 c

Moving beyond the Hamburger Approach

Although the way feedback is given and received can be influenced by cultural factors and individual preferences, these are also changing as globalised management training programmes and multinational corporations bring their own approaches to employees around the world. Some of those on the receiving end of the Hamburger Approach have also become savvy to it and are starting to question the authenticity of the praise, preferring feedback givers to just get to the point.

However, the culture of feedback can sometimes be more complex than the simple hamburger.

 ## The culture of feedback

When approaching a new feedback culture, consider the following variables and how these might change depending on the context and type of feedback:

- How much positive feedback is expected? How should it be delivered?
- How much negative feedback is expected? How should it be delivered?
- Who can you give direct feedback to?
  - People you know well vs people you don't know very well?
  - Subordinates vs superiors vs peers?
- When is an appropriate time to give feedback?
  - In private (one-to-one) vs in front of others?
  - In a formal appraisal vs an informal chat?
  - When it is solicited vs when it is unsolicited?
- What medium should feedback be given in?
  - Written or spoken?
  - If written, who should be cc-ed in?

Approaching feedback with a growth mindset

Ultimately, the goal of feedback is to encourage growth and development, and to pinpoint areas for improvement. Stanford Psychologist Carol Dweck[35] proposed that the way we give feedback could serve to either encourage a *growth mindset* (where talents can be developed through hard work, good strategies and support from others) or perpetuate a *fixed mindset* (where people believe that intelligence and talent are fixed traits i.e. you are either good or bad at something and there is little you can do to change that).

---

35 Dweck CS (2008) *Mindset: The new psychology of success.* New York: Ballantine Books.

Compliments and positive feedback should not only be given to sugar coat the negatives, but should be offered to reinforce and encourage good performance. Instead of focusing our praise merely on results, consider also praising the efforts and improvements made, the strategies used, the persistence with challenging tasks, the resourcefulness and the willingness to experiment. Positive feedback like, *'You must have worked really hard to accomplish this!'* can stimulate a growth mindset and encourage progress.

Leaders with a growth mindset recognise that mistakes and failures are essential to learning and improving, and they need to be accepted as part of the developmental process. Giving developmental feedback is not therefore seen as passing judgment or evaluation of another's performance, but a way of helping them grow.

Being objective about the past, and focusing on the future

By focusing on solutions and ways of doing things differently in the future, rather than getting into a tirade of *'should haves'* and *'could haves'*, we can move the focus from the past onto the future, offering *feed forward*[36] instead of *feedback*. After all, the receiver of the feedback cannot change the past. Instead, we can help them see the opportunities that the past offers to help them improve on the future.

Understandably, we cannot ignore the things that have gone wrong in the past. But by being specific and using objective language that describes the facts rather than using emotional and subjective language that judges and making sweeping evaluations, we can avoid demoralising the receiver and instead engage them with finding a solution to the problem or an improvement to the situation.

One way of doing this is to use the SBI tool[37] when giving feedback. With a focus on facts and observations rather than emotions and judgments, the SBI tool enables us to remove the sugar coating process in feedback (the buns of the Hamburger model), and be honest and direct without being offensive to the receiver.

---

36 Goldsmith M (2012) *Feedforward*. Writer of the Round Table Press.

37 Developed by the Centre for Creative Leadership. See: https://www.ccl.org/lead-it-yourself-solutions/ workshop-kits/feedback-that-works/ (accessed September 2018).

The SBI Tool

Situation: the SBI tool suggests that we structure feedback by first defining the situation and the setting, and providing the context, e.g. *'You were in charge of organising yesterday's launch event ...,'*

Behaviour: We then go on to objectively describe the specific behaviour that was observed, e.g. *'You invited a lot of political journalists to attend the event. They weren't quite the target market for our new technological device.'*

Impact: Outline how this behaviour had an impact on you or on others, e.g. *'I don't think they understood the product we were launching or what it was supposed to do, and as a result, we might not get the publicity we were aiming for.'*

Next steps: Allow the receiver to reflect on the feedback that has been given, and discuss the necessary improvements and changes that needs to take place for the future, e.g. *'For future launches, how can we more accurately target our invitations so that we get an audience that appreciates our product more?'*

Encouraging development through feedback

Whichever tool or model we decide to use, feedback that falls on deaf ears is not going to result in development. We need to engage the receiver and help them view the feedback as developmental. By using questions when offering developmental feedback, the receiver can be guided to reflect and become aware of these developmental opportunities.

 ## Development feedback

Consider questions like the following when offering developmental feedback:

- What happened? (Describe the problem.)
- Why do you think this might be a problem? (Describe the impact of the problem.)
- What do you think we can do to avoid this happening in the future?

- **How do you think you can solve this problem if it happens again in the future?**
- **What do you think you can improve on?**
- **How do you think you can develop this?**
- **What can I do to help you improve on this?**
- **What support might you need to develop on this?**

In order for your employees to buy in to the developmental potential that feedback can offer, it is crucial that managers and leaders create a feedback culture in the team/organisation where they themselves set the example of welcoming constructive feedback. By giving staff the opportunity to suggest ways for their manager(s) to improve, they are demonstrating a receptiveness and an acceptance that we all have areas that we can work on. Whether the feedback is delivered face to face in your office or in a written email, ensure that employees know that you are genuinely asking for their feedback and not simply paying lip service to the concept.

Communicate this culture of openness with your team by talking about the growth mindset and the importance of feedback. Encourage peer feedback in order to support each other's development and nurture an environment where your staff becomes comfortable in asking for feedback both from their managers and their peers.

It is by talking honestly about the role of feedback and the way it is given and received that we can stop tiptoeing around this often-dreaded area and start embracing it as a tool for individual and organisational growth.

Chapter 8: Influencing

Influencing skills

One of the tools I often use on my communication skills courses is roleplay. During these sessions I often found myself learning a lot simply by observing the different influencing skills my participants would call on when roleplaying a negotiation.

Interestingly, less experienced negotiators tended to use more forceful methods like coercion, manipulation, bullying or even nagging to get their way. These negotiations were the ones that often ended most quickly, with the participants deciding there was no way out of their situation and parting without a satisfactory agreement, or with one party giving up or giving in due to sheer exhaustion and exasperation. There was almost no doubt that in a real-life situation, a prolonged relationship and repeat business for these participants would almost certainly be out of the question. In contrast, the more experienced participants often demonstrated a wider range of skills, making use of logical reasoning, emotional appeals and rapport to win over their counterparts.

Then one day, Sven, a confident man in his 50s, turned up on my course and tackled every single negotiation roleplay with finesse, persuading every single participant to his way of thinking and into giving him what he wanted. Sven won over each and every person he negotiated with by adjusting his influencing style to suit them, interacting with them so that they felt understood and involved in the decisions made, and making them feel that he had done his best to meet them at least half way.

It turned out that Sven conducted large-scale negotiations for a living and was well-versed in the art of influencing people from diverse backgrounds. He was able to get them to change their minds and/or get them to act in a certain way while maintaining their relationship by employing a range of influencing skills he had honed over many years.

So, what are influencing skills and why are they important? Traditionally, in a more hierarchical society, the people who wield the most power, and therefore the most influence, are the ones in authority and those with a high status or position in society. With globalisation and the rise of online platforms there has been a move towards flatter hierarchical structures where the power is in the hands of those who have the skills to influence behaviour, change minds and get things done. Whether it is because you are managing a team of diverse people, negotiating a deal or trying to convince management of your ideas, having influencing skills means that you are able to achieve results.

Push and pull

The dichotomous model of push and pull influencing styles is one that perhaps exemplifies the difference between the more top-down approach and the more collaborative bottom-up approach to influencing, although both styles are sometimes used in combination.

So what is the difference between the two approaches? An influencer using a push style might state their own suggestion or opinion, and then attempt to move the listener towards their point of view by offering reasons as to why the suggestion is a good one or why the influencer is correct. The listener is thus 'pushed' into agreeing with the influencer. Conversely, an influencer using a pull style might ask the listener for their ideas and suggestions, ask questions to explore and develop the ideas, before deciding on a way forward together.

 Look at the arguments below and decide which of the boxes (A, B, C, or D) belong to the push style of influencing and which belong to the pull style. Think also about the different styles in each case.

A	B
'So what do you think about this?'	*'Here's my take on the situation.'*
'And why do you think this is the case?'	*'These statistics clearly show that...'*
'What's the most important thing for you here?'	*'The market is ready for this.'*
'What would you be willing to accept?'	*'If you look at the facts, you'll see that...'*
'What would be a ideal solution for you?'	*'In my experience...'*

C	D
'Listen, I've got a great idea.'	'What are our different options here?'
'Wouldn't it be amazing if...?'	'What are the advantages and disadvantages of doing it this way?'
'I think you'll love this.'	
'You know in your heart that this is the best way forward.'	'Do you think the pros outweigh the cons in this case?'
'I think we would struggle to find a better option.'	'How can we overcome those drawbacks?'
	'Would you say that this is the best option too?'

Boxes B and C both feature a push style of influencing, as they feature phrases used to convince the listener and move them towards an idea or suggestion that the influencer has. However, they display different levels of assertiveness and a different focus in pitch. Column B attempts to *push* an idea onto the listener using reasoning, facts, the experience and/or status of the influencer, while box C employs interpersonal skills such as rapport, trust, friendliness and an insight into the listener's emotions to *push* the idea across. If you are confident that your ideas/proposals are good, you may have quick success with a push style of influencing. However, if you feel your ideas may still need some development, then a more collaborative pull approach could be more suited.

Boxes A and D feature a pull style of influencing, as they both make use of questions to explore the listener's take on the matter. However, in box A there is an open use of questions to embrace the listener's wants and needs so as to collaboratively figure out a solution. This is contrasted with a more systematic exploration of co-identifying the pros and cons of each option in box D.

Other influencing styles

In addition to the push and pull model, there are several frameworks that use different ways of breaking the art of influencing down to its smaller parts. *Forbes* magazine[38] groups influencing styles into the following five useful categories:

- Asserting.
- Convincing.
- Negotiating.
- Bridging.
- Inspiring.

 Think about the times when you had to persuade or influence someone. Do you have a dominant default style? If so, which of the following descriptions corresponds most closely to it?

A. **Asserting Style:** Resonating with the push style of influencing, this asserting style requires the influencer to have confidence in their proposals and judgments and firmly persists in the face of opposition, without being aggressive.

B. **Convincing Style:** Making use of reasoning, facts, statistics and data, this style makes use of logical and analytical thinking to convince others of your point of view. (See ➔ 'Holistic vs analytical ways of thinking' on page 133.)

C. **Negotiating Style:** An ability to discuss terms and make compromises and concessions can help all parties reach a satisfactory agreement. This also requires an understanding of your alternatives and the ultimate goals and targets that you're trying to achieve.

D. **Bridging Style:** The use of interpersonal skills to create strong bonds and collaboration between all parties can show others that their opinions and ideas are being valued and build a strong relationship for both present and future co-operation.

E. **Inspiring Style:** This style focuses on enthusing others to share your vision and your excitement for the desired behaviour or outcome and motivates them to invest (emotionally and otherwise) in your goals.

---

38 Based on research conducted by Discovery Inc. and Innovative Pathways in 2009 and 2010. See: https://www.forbes.com/sites/work-in-progress/2011/12/21/five-steps-to-increase-your-influence/#3dfe22d1372c (accessed September 2018).

> Did you recognise your dominant influencing style there? Does the influencing style you employ change depending on the situation and your goals? Perhaps you use a more asserting style when you are in a higher position of status, or when you do not have to pay careful attention to the relationship you have with the other party. Perhaps you use a more convincing style when you're trying to get the others to buy into a certain theory or way of thinking, and a bridging style to decide on what restaurant to go to for your team night out. The more flexible we are and the more aware we are of our goals, the more we are able to adapt our influencing style to suit the different circumstances and the people we meet.

Holistic vs analytical ways of thinking

I like telling stories and sharing experiences and lessons learnt through anecdotes. I sometimes find them to be a great way of making a point and bringing people round to my way of thinking without being overly pushy … and I guess this comes through in my writing as well.

When I tell stories, I find it vital to set the scene, and I often spend time building the context for the listener. Every detail is important because they play a role in the way we interpret the subsequent story, but this need to paint an accurate backdrop to my story might not always go down well with my listeners. Once or twice, close friends have voiced their confusion at the relevance of some of those details, wondering why I don't get to my point sooner (perhaps a little like the way this anecdote is unfolding right now). Things don't exist in isolation though, and from my perspective, certain points can't be made without presenting the bigger picture first.

This can be described as a holistic way of thinking that is said to often characterise certain Eastern cultures. Defined as a tendency to see everything as a whole and not just a sum of its parts[39] – a holistic way of thinking connects the world, nature, society, humans and their behaviour, etc. – all of which complement each other to form a larger picture.

---

39 Bertalanffy L (1968) *General Systems Theory, Foundation, Development, Application*. New York: G. Braziller.

Researchers have in recent years been looking into holism as a framework for understanding cultural differences, and psychologists Huang and Park[40] discovered that profile pictures on the popular social media platform Facebook provided an interesting example of the East Asian tendency towards holistic thinking. In two studies that examined more than 3,500 Facebook profile pictures, they discovered that while Americans preferred to display profile photos of their faces (with details of their smiles and facial expressions), East Asians from Taiwan, Hong Kong and Singapore were more likely to use profile pictures that included more information about their background and environment, with less emphasis on their faces.

Facebook profile photos

In another experiment, this time by Masuda and Nisbett[41], American and Japanese subjects were asked to take photos of a person. The Americans seemed to prefer close-ups of the individual while the Japanese tended to take photos that showed the person in his/her environment. In a separate experiment, their subjects were presented with a short animated video clip of underwater scenes and were then asked to describe what they had been shown. While the Americans seemed preoccupied with the objects in the foreground, the Japanese seemed to focus more on objects in the background and how they co-related to the objects in the foreground.

40 Huang CH & Park D (2013) Cultural influences on Facebook photographs. *International Journal of Psychology* **8** p334–343

41 Masuda T & Nisbett RA (2001) Attending holistically versus analytically: comparing the context sensitivity of Japanese and Americans. *Journal of Personality and Social Psychology* **8** p922–934.

Reflecting the more Western values of individuality, autonomy and freedom of expression, the more analytical way of thinking (aka *specific thinking*) allows the examination of an object out of its environment and the attributing of causes to individual agents. In contrast, values such as group harmony, group loyalty, co-operation and duty towards the family and the community (many of them borne out of Confucian values) underlie the holistic way of thinking, viewing everything and everyone as interconnected and interdependent on each other.

People with a holistic way of thinking thus tend to see their role in a team/ organisation/community as contributing to a larger scheme of things, complementing each other to achieve a greater goal. Also seeing words as part of a larger setting when communicating, it is not uncommon for Eastern cultures to place emphasis on context, relationships and experience-based knowledge[42], also often known as a high context style of communication. (See ➔ 'Cultural frameworks and dimensions' on page 33 and 'Directness' on page 83 for more on high vs low context communication.) However, for someone with a more analytical style of thinking, a holistic thinker who employs a high context style of communication might sometimes come across as indirect, unclear, and even confusing.

 In the following critical incident, Yipei is trying to influence her manager, Fred, but is doing it in a way that is unfamiliar to Fred. Imagine you were Fred and decide which of the four options you would pick.

Fred was in charge of an international project team and found dealing with Yipei particularly exhausting. Take for example the time when he tried to get her on board with the new reporting system that required team members to prepare a weekly report for their Wednesday team meetings. Yipei seemed reluctant and so Fred called her into his office for a face-to-face chat about her reservations. Yipei started talking about the importance of developing professionally and not becoming complacent with her IT skills. Fred could not understand why she was changing the subject and tried to ask her how she felt about reporting back every Wednesday. Yipei responded by talking about how grateful she was that the company was sending her on an evening IT course and how much she was enjoying the opportunity to grow. Fred found her responses puzzling and wasn't sure how to respond.

The four options he considered were:
A. not pursue the matter any further
B. ask Yipei what her evening classes had to do with the weekly reports
C. look into Yipei's evening IT classes that the company was sending her on
D. reprimand Yipei for not answering his questions and insist on a direct response: i.e. a 'yes' or 'no' to weekly reports.

42 Ibid.

If you were Fred, how would you have chosen to deal with Yipei's responses? Read the results of your choice below.

If you chose (a):

When it came to their Wednesday team meetings, Yipei turned up unprepared and gave inadequate reports of her week that were lacking in statistical detail. She often looked tired and annoyed at the meetings, but Fred continued to ignore the situation and their relationship grew strained.

If you chose (b):

Fred continued to ask for clarification, saying, 'I'm not sure if I understand you completely. How are your evening classes connected to the weekly reports?' Yipei started saying how important it was for her to prepare her weekly reports and how much time it would take to consolidate the statistics. She would have been happy to stay late on Tuesday evenings to do the preparation but that was the evening her weekly IT course took place. After considering the circumstances, Fred asked if moving the team report meetings to Thursdays would help. Yipei was very grateful and ensured that she prepped for her weekly reports with great care and attention.

If you chose (c):

Fred looked into the company's employee records and saw that Yipei's IT classes took place every Tuesday evening from 6.30pm to 10.30pm. He also found out that Yipei lived an hour's drive away from the city centre where the office and her classes were based. Realising that Yipei might be concerned about her ability to prepare for a weekly report by Wednesday morning, Fred asked her if she would prefer it if the team meetings were on Thursday mornings instead. Yipei was pleased that Fred followed up on the issue and voiced her appreciation of Fred's suggestion, promising she would be well-prepared for the report meetings on Thursdays.

If you chose (d):

Fred got annoyed and told Yipei off for not answering his questions directly. He demanded to know on the spot if she was for the weekly reports or not and she said she was. However, when Yipei turned up at the meetings unprepared, Fred saw that as an inability to deliver. Yipei stopped communicating with him and their relationship grew strained.

To someone like Fred, who had an analytical way of thinking and tended to prefer getting 'to the point' and narrowing down issues to a direct cause and effect, Yipei's way of talking might seem unclear and confusing. The idiom 'beating round the bush' came to mind when he thought of Yipei's way of communicating.

In contrast, Yipei felt she was being very clear. In her holistic way of thinking, everything is interconnected: her commitment to the IT classes was her way of showing her appreciation for the professional development the company was providing her with, but this commitment would impact upon her ability to deliver at the Wednesday meetings. In her high context style of communication, Yipei also assumed that as her line manager, Fred would be up to date about her professional development, but in order to avoid causing him to lose face, she was careful not to speak in a way that assumed Fred's ignorance of her Tuesday evening classes.

When dealing with communication issues, I've often noticed that both parties are frequently insistent that they had been very clear and that it should be obvious what they were trying to say. Yet from the other's perspective, the message might have been buried under different conventions. Whether it is due to different ways of thinking or different styles of communication, it is important not to make assumptions based on our own cultural filters and to ask questions when in any doubt.

Deductive or inductive reasoning?

Imagine you want to persuade your client to part with their money and buy your product. How do you persuade them? Consider the following two paths of persuasion.

Reasoning pathways

Path D	Path I
Path D You point out that many companies have been suffering a loss of income due to X.	**Path I** You point out that many companies have been suffering a loss of income due to X.
Thesis You bring up the research into Y, a possible solution for X: its parameters, and the statistics it yielded.	**Observations & examples** You bring up examples of how some companies have used Y to solve X and the results they got (and an implied understanding that X can be solved by Y).
Anti-thesis You address the potential issues with Y.	
Synthesis You show how X can be solved by Y.	**Applications** You suggest strategies for applying Y to X.
Conclusion You emphasise why Y is the solution your client needs for X.	**Conclusion** You emphasise why Y is the solution your client needs for X.

Path D uses deductive reasoning: positing a hypothesis (Y is a possible solution for X), forming a thesis, an anti-thesis and a synthesis where eventually a specific conclusion is reached. The argument is built from general (theory) to specifics (the application).

Path I uses inductive reasoning: first offering specific observations, examples and applications based on the real world, and from the generalisations, assuming that a conclusion may be drawn (therefore Y is a solution for X).

Using the terms principles-first reasoning (Path D) and applications-first reasoning (Path I), author of *The Culture Map*, Erin Meyer, suggests that Anglo-Saxon cultures like the US, UK, Australia, Canada etc. tend to prefer a inductive style of reasoning, and this could possibly be traced back to the methodologies of British thinkers like Roger Bacon, Francis Bacon and the American pioneers' move away from theoretical learning[43].

---

43 Erin Meyer (2014) *The Culture Map*. United States of America: Public Affairs.

Countries like Italy, France, Russia, Spain and Germany on the other hand seem to display a preference for deductive reasoning (albeit to different extents), perhaps originating from the preferred methods of European philosophers like Descartes and Hegel.

Attempting to persuade someone who is used to a different way of thinking from your own can be tricky and could result in some unexpected reactions.

Consider the following reactions. Which statements are typically said by someone who is used to deductive reasoning? And which of them are typically said by someone used to inductive reasoning?

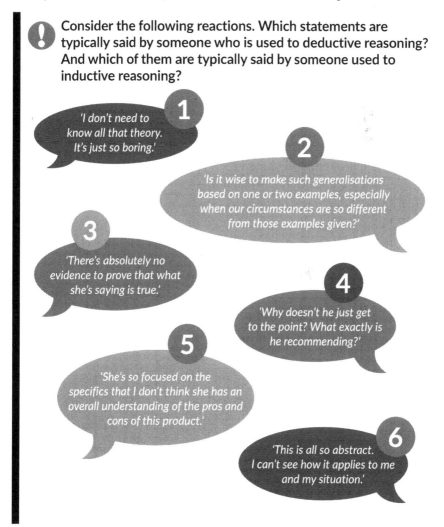

1 'I don't need to know all that theory. It's just so boring.'

2 'Is it wise to make such generalisations based on one or two examples, especially when our circumstances are so different from those examples given?'

3 'There's absolutely no evidence to prove that what she's saying is true.'

4 'Why doesn't he just get to the point? What exactly is he recommending?'

5 'She's so focused on the specifics that I don't think she has an overall understanding of the pros and cons of this product.'

6 'This is all so abstract. I can't see how it applies to me and my situation.'

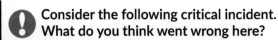

Answers: Statements 1, 4 and 6 could be said by someone used to inductive reasoning speaking about someone who is using deductive reasoning. Statements 2, 3 and 5 could be said by someone used to deductive reasoning and speaking about someone who is using inductive reasoning.

The ability to see how others might subscribe to a different way of reasoning could help us frame the way we perceive their attempts to influence us and perhaps help us avoid the type of judgments and conclusions that the above speakers came to. It would also hopefully urge us to consider the suitability of the methods we use when trying to influence someone and how we might be better able to tailor our strategies to appeal to the other party's preferred style of reasoning so as to achieve the results we desire.

However, attempts to respond positively can sometimes be interpreted differently from what was intended.

Consider the following critical incident. What do you think went wrong here?

Ed is in a meeting presenting his business idea to Katrin.

Ed: *So what do you think?*

Katrin: *Yes, but the problem is the low profit margin.*

Ed: *I see. We can double the price.*

Katrin: *Ok, but there is the problem of the production cost.*

Ed: *We can always change to a cheaper material.*

Katrin: *Yes, but then the problem is the target market won't buy the product.*

Ed: *Maybe we can change the product and target a different market?*

When Ed heard Katrin react to them with the words 'the problem is ...', he immediately interpreted it as a rejection of what he had suggested. Desperate to sell his idea, he started to modify his original proposal to suit Katrin, not realising that in fact Katrin's use of the phrase 'the problem is ...' merely indicated her interest in the proposal and her desire to explore it further (the 'anti-thesis' stage of the deductive reasoning process). By constantly amending his proposal, Ed has instead come across as uncertain and unconvinced of the viability of what he himself was suggesting.

This critical incident clearly illustrates that interpretations of meaning are often based on our assumptions and our own understanding of the world. While we might speak the same language, the very same words might not carry the same meaning for all of us and sometimes explicit clarification is needed to achieve mutual understanding.

When trying to persuade someone, it is important that we do not simply consider our own way of thinking and how we ourselves would like to be influenced. Perhaps knowledge of Katrin's possible preference for deductive reasoning and her direct way of communication might have led Ed to consider different interpretations to Katrin's words, and prevented him from jumping in with his modifications. A successful influencer is able to put themselves in the position of those they would like to influence, and tailor their strategy and communication style accordingly.

Other cultural considerations

When communicating internationally, what other factors could affect your attempt to influence someone's decisions, way of thinking or behaviour?

 Here are some cultural dimensions previously mentioned (see → Chapter 2) that are worth considering.

Match the tips in the right column to the interlocutors in the left column.

Long-term orientation vs short-term orientation	
1. *Influencing someone with long-term orientation.*	(a) Focus on traditions, experience and past results. When trying to initiate change, look for examples from the past that can serve as evidence. Make an effort with references made to history and past achievements as these could go down well.
2. *Influencing someone with short-term orientation.*	(b) Focus on how the change would have a positive effect on the future. Where possible, paint your vision of the future and consider how what you are suggesting can lead to improvement, growth and advancement.

High power distance vs low power distance

3. *Influencing someone used to higher power distance.*	**(c)** Pay attention to the chain of command and the organisational hierarchy. It might be necessary to use more formal language when communicating, especially in written communication such as emails.
4. *Influencing someone used to lower power distance.*	It might help to also consider how your status in your company corresponds to theirs. When trying to influence someone of higher status than you, it might work better if you took on a more deferential and restrained manner as opposed to being over-enthusiastic, over-confident and assertive. Those of a lower status might not have the power to make the decisions you require. **(d)** Do not assume that their managers are fully informed of their actions and whereabouts. They might have the authority to make decisions on their own without consulting their superiors. They might also communicate directly with people above and below your chain of command without any intention of disrespecting you or the organisational hierarchy. If the person you are trying to influence is someone you manage, allow for more autonomy, ask them questions about what they think and how they feel, and do not expect them to agree with you just because of your authoritative position.

Relationship orientation vs task orientation

5. *Influencing someone who is more relationship-oriented.*	**(e)** You can build trust by demonstrating your experience and competence when working side by side. By overcoming challenges and attaining your goals together, you can build strong, lasting relationships.
6. *Influencing someone who is more task-oriented.*	Understand that they might prefer to draw a line between their professional and personal lives and might not have the time or see the need for socialising outside work. In conversations, show a more professional side and, when offering your views, try to include objective as well as personal ones.

(f) Consider the importance of spending time developing your relationship as this could affect the influence you would have on them.

This could mean allowing time for small talk and/or socialising outside the office e.g. having dinner or drinks, where you might share personal information, ideas and opinions that might reveal the kind of person you are. Avoid rushing the business side of things before trust is built or you might risk losing their attention completely.

Answer key: 1 (b); 2 (a); 3 (c); 4 (d); 5 (f); 6 (e)

Putting our influencing skills to practice

There are many factors that could affect how we could or should go about influencing someone, and those listed above are by no means all of them. Like any other skill, influencing is one that gets better with practice. However, we do not have to wait for the occasion to take part in an important pitch or a large-scale negotiation in order to practise our influencing skills. Opportunities to practise our influencing skills happen around us all the time: getting a better deal at a market stall, asking your boss to get the department a new microwave, convincing our colleague to do us a favour, arguing about the environment over a cup of coffee with our friends, persuading our colleagues (or family members) to change their mind about a decision they've made. We try to influence the people around us all the time. We can do this while consciously reflecting on the strategies we use and how those might change depending on who we are speaking to and what we are speaking about. Only then can we start to hone this important skill and prepare ourselves for the influencing we need to do when communicating internationally.

Chapter 9: Conflict management

What is conflict and why does it exist?

Gloria, the head of HR based in Venezuela, was giving a presentation to her colleagues suggesting ways of cutting their HR budget. Unconvinced, Freja started to question some of Gloria's ideas, making what she thought were helpful counter-proposals in an effort to reduce the cuts' impact on the staff. Gloria felt that Freja's open disagreements represented a personal attack that embarrassed her in front of her colleagues but when she saw Freja the next day, she was surprised that Freja continued behaving in the same friendly way as if nothing had happened between them.

Meanwhile in India, Chris and Kumar were experiencing a different problem. Chris was an external consultant brought in to deal with the issues Kumar's team was having. One afternoon when Kumar was out meeting a client, Chris noticed that one of Kumar's team members was having trouble with the new technology and decided to sit down with him to work through his issues. When Kumar heard what had happened behind his back, he was furious. Chris had failed to go through what were the proper channels in Kumar's eyes, and dealt with a team member directly instead of going through Kumar. Kumar felt that Chris was purposely undermining his power in a political move. However, when he brought up the incident it was clear from Chris's confused look that Chris had no idea there was anything wrong.

In the two cases above, both Gloria and Kumar were convinced that friction had arisen between them and their co-worker. This perceived friction led to ill feelings, anger and upset, and they believed they were in a conflict situation, only to realise that Freja and Chris were both oblivious to the existence of any conflict.

Conflict can arise when there is a disagreement, argument or clash about something that is important, but as we can see in the examples above, it isn't always clear to all parties involved that a conflict exists. Conflict is not uncommon in the workplace, and certainly not uncommon when communicating internationally. In fact, every single critical incident in this book illustrates a type of conflict.

Many managers and team leaders spend a good proportion of their time managing issues of conflict. After all, conflict that is not dealt with can have negative consequences and create problems in working together. However, when conflict is handled well, it can lead to mutual understanding, increased trust and improved relationships, enhanced self-awareness, and a better ability to communicate openly and effectively. Whether you are a manager or a team member, the ability to manage conflict well is one that could help you surmount problems and build better relationships with your colleagues and your business associates.

Identifying the source of conflict

The first step to resolving conflict is the ability to identify the source of the problem. In Art Bell[44] and Brett Hart's[45] studies of workplace conflict, they collectively suggested that conflict could be reduced to these eight causes.

❶ Conflicting resources

Arguments about how money is spent and how time is used are not just confined to the workplace. They are common causes of conflict in families as well. Resources are finite and everyone wants to have a say as to how they are used. It is important that the parties involved are able to prioritise their needs and negotiate to find a solution that works for everyone.

❷ Conflicting styles

Different working styles, different practices and different ways of seeing or doing things can cause issues, especially when the other party is unable to understand the reasons for things being done differently. Gloria and Freja, for example, had different ideas as to how disagreement should be handled. While Gloria felt that Freja should have been more discreet and offered her counter proposals in a more private setting, Freja saw her actions as part of a healthy debate that could lead to better team outcomes.

An open conversation about each other's styles can not only lead to a better understanding, but also enables both parties to learn to be more flexible and accepting of ways that differ from their own. If the conflict is within a team, it might help to clarify the expected processes and practices of the team.

44 Bell A (2002) *Six Ways to Resolve Workplace Conflicts*. San Francisco, C.A.: University of San Francisco.

45 Hart B (2009) *Conflict in the Workplace. Behavioural Consultants*, P.C. http://www.excelatlife.com/articles/conflict_at_work.htm (accessed September 2018).

❸ Conflicting perceptions

We cannot assume that everyone is working based on the same information. Whether it is due to different sets of instructions, recent news about a client or hearsay about a situation, increased knowledge is likely to affect the way we perceive something and perhaps change the way we work with it. If two parties are privy to different information, they might see things differently and conflict might ensue. An open dialogue can help shed light on the different perspectives.

❹ Conflicting goals

It would be ideal if people who were working together were also working towards a common goal. However, in reality this does not always happen. Two parties in a negotiation might come to the table with very different agendas, members of the same project team might have allegiances to the goals of their different departments or different branches, and individuals might have their own personal targets in mind. This can make working together difficult, especially if all parties are under the assumption or pretense of having the same goals. So consider revisiting goals and targets when possible to ensure everyone is on the same page.

❺ Conflicting pressures

Everyday working life can be filled with the stress of deadlines, urgent tasks and impromptu requests. If more work piles on our desk when we are already pushed to our limits to deliver, this can lead to resentment and anger. This can sometimes be resolved by a better mutual understanding of the long- and short-term objectives and schedules of parties involved.

❻ Conflicting roles

It can be disconcerting when our understanding of our roles in an organisation/team are being challenged by parties who encroach on areas we had thought we were responsible for. In the example above, Kumar had operated on the belief that it was solely his job to train and communicate with his team members. In his view, Chris had overstepped his boundary by dealing with his team member directly, thus undermining his authority and disrespecting his role as team leader. Chris, on the other hand, came from a culture (national, corporate or otherwise) where it was acceptable – and in fact efficient practice – to deal with individuals directly as an external consultant, and saw it as his responsibility to help out. By communicating about the issue, both parties can better understand each other's roles and responsibilities and how and why they are assigned as such.

❼ Different personal values

As we have seen from the examples in this book (for instance, see ➔ the Cultural Iceberg on page 31), our values and beliefs often underlie our behaviour and practices. When we are faced with behaviour that stems from a different set of beliefs or when we are asked to act in a way that goes against our values, it can be difficult to understand, and this can result in conflict. The start of conflict management begins with a self-awareness of how our behaviour is affected by our values and beliefs, and an ability to communicate our feelings clearly and calmly when we are faced with tasks or behaviour that conflict with our values.

❽ Unpredictable policies

We live in a world of constant change, and when teams span across boundaries and business is done internationally, we are not always able to keep up with the latest government or corporate policies. When changes in policies are not communicated properly, different people may operate under different assumptions and this can lead to conflicting perceptions. It is therefore important that when policies change we understand how and why they are changing, and this can only happen through clear communication.

In the varying causes of conflict above, the suggested resolutions have advocated approaching conflict in an open way and prioritised using clear and effective communication. However, not everyone deals with conflict in the same way and sometimes different situations might call for a different approaches.

Approaches to conflict

Once we have recognised the cause, we can start to deal with the points of conflict. However, the way we choose to deal with conflict might also differ. Kenneth Thomas and Ralph Kilmann identified two basic dimensions of behaviour when dealing with conflict: assertiveness and co-operativeness. This gives rise to a further five different conflict management modes[46].

While some seem to interpret these five modes as a representation of five different personality types, Thomas and Kilmann themselves suggest that while some of us might use some modes better than others and have a dominant style, we are all capable of each of the following five modes and are unlikely to have just one single way of dealing with conflict.

---

46 http://www.kilmanndiagnostics.com/overview-thomas-kilmann-conflict-mode-instrument-tki (accessed September 2018).

Having the flexibility to adopt different styles of conflict management can help us tailor our style to suit different circumstances, different people and different issues. An understanding of these different modes can also allow us to recognise the conflict management styles of the people we are dealing with, and enable us to better appreciate their attitudes and feelings towards the conflict.

Consider the Conflict Mode Instrument and how each mode is described below. Which mode do you relate to most?

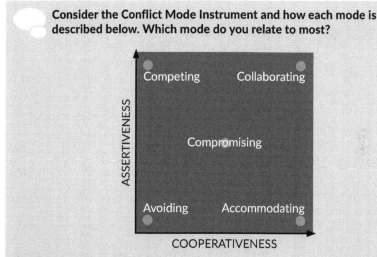

The Thomas-Kilmann Conflict Mode Instrument

The **Competition Mode** is all about trying to win at all costs. It is high on assertiveness and low on co-operativeness, and assumes a win-lose outcome where one party wins and the others lose. This power-oriented style of dealing with conflict could be a result of a lack of understanding of the other parties, a feeling of not being heard or that one needs to stand up for their beliefs, or a defensive reaction towards what is happening.

Conversely, high on co-operativeness but low on assertiveness is the **Accommodation Mode**. By giving in to the needs and demands of the more assertive party, the 'accommodator' sacrifices their own in order to keep the peace and avoid further confrontation. This style could lead to unresolved issues and to the more assertive parties taking charge.

Taking a more moderate position on assertiveness and co-operativeness is the **Compromise Mode**. The situation is addressed, and a middle ground is found for all those involved. Concessions are made on both sides and everyone is partially happy that their needs are partially met. While this mode is time-efficient, it does not allow for detailed exploring of both sides of the story and the alternative solutions available to them.

The **Avoiding Mode**, being low on assertiveness and low on co-operativeness, is characterised by a preference for avoiding the conflict completely and withdrawing from the situation or changing the subject and sidestepping the problem in hope that it would go away. Like the Accommodation Mode, avoidance, in some situations, could lead to unresolved issues, which if left to fester could become potentially toxic for the relationship.

When a person is keen to satisfy both his goals and the other parties', he might go into **Collaboration Mode** and try to find a win-win solution by having an open dialogue, learning from points of disagreement and looking for a creative solution that can ensure that the needs of both parties are fulfilled. The in-depth exploration of the Collaboration Mode means that it would often take more time and effort to elicit and listen to the different aspects of the issue than the above modes.

Do you have a dominant style when it comes to managing the conflict in your life, or are you comfortable using different approaches depending on the people and the situations you are in?

Consider the following potential conflicts. How do you think you might approach these situations? Which of the above five modes might you use in each of them? Write down your approach in the space given.

1   Your colleague Jess wants you to join her for lunch with her client today. It isn't your client and you would prefer to spend the time catching up on your emails. But Jess is insisting that your presence would help her in her negotiations with the client.

2   Your name is Deborah but Lee from the finance department keeps calling you Debbie and you really don't like that nickname.

3   Your counterpart in the head office on the other side of the globe has a habit of calling you at 2am once a month for your department reports.

4   You're about to close an important deal with a client from Kazakhstan. Your husband/wife works closely with the Kazakh government but this has never come up in conversation before. Your manager suggests that you mention this in your next meeting as it might get the client to sign the contract more quickly. You don't find this necessary or ethical.

5   You often find that when you come back to your desk in the morning, things have been moved around and are not always easy to find. You realise that a colleague working a different shift has been using your desk in the evenings.

6   Your team member often CCs your manager in all your email communication with him. Your manager then gets involved in all the smaller decisions that you make. You find this unnecessary and it sometimes affects the way you deal with certain issues.

7   You hear from your manager that a colleague has voiced an issue with the way you clock out of the office at 5pm every day despite the fact that many of your colleagues work overtime till 9pm almost every night. You have family obligations and you had assumed that your colleagues know that.

8   Two months ago your company approved your request to reduce your number of working days from five to three days a week along with a reduced salary. However, you have noticed that your workload has stayed the same and your manager now expects you to complete the same amount of work in a shorter amount of time. This has proved strenuous, and every time your manager reprimands you for another deadline you have missed, your stress and anger levels increase.

Looking at your responses to the above scenarios, do you have a default approach to handling conflict? Are there other ways of looking at the situations? What might the other party's perspective be?

Arguably there are no right or wrong solutions to the scenarios above. You might find some of the situations to be non-issues and it would be simpler if you gave in or paid no notice to them. You might find that the way you deal with the conflict depends largely on how important it is for you to preserve the relationship at hand.

But if your default position consistently tends to be one of avoidance, or conversely one of confrontational emotional outbursts, then it might be useful to consider the consequences of having such a conflict management style, especially when working internationally. Ask yourself these questions: does your default style effectively manage the conflict? Would you end up getting what you want? Would your relationship be in jeopardy as a result?

Communicating in conflict situations

Sometimes a conflict situation is in need of a resolution and cannot (or should not) be swept under the carpet and ignored. And in order to deal with the issue without damaging the relationship, communication is key: we need to be able to discuss the problem so as to resolve the issue… and sometimes an open dialogue is the resolution in itself. However, communication during a conflict can be tricky and a well-meaning conversation can exacerbate a situation. In trying to get our point across, we sometimes say things that do not help matters.

 Sonja is trying to talk to her teammate Richard in order to resolve an issue she has with him. Consider the impact of the words of both parties. What might you advise Sonja and Richard to do differently?

Sonja: *I have a real issue with the fact that you never mean what you say.*

Richard: *What are you talking about?*

Sonja: *You said we would work on the social media report together but yesterday, when I asked you for help with it, you were so reluctant.*

Richard: *That is so not true.*

Sonja: *If you don't want to help, then don't be fake and pretend that you're so helpful. It's dishonest. And you do this all the time … like that time, in front of the boss, when you pretended to be such a team player and …*

Richard: *I'm not dishonest and I do want to help. It's just extremely difficult to work with you because you are always so negative.*

Sonja: *That's such rubbish.*

Richard: *Whenever I try to help you, you pick fault with everything I do. 'This is not the right way! Do it like that! Don't do it like that!' You're a control freak and you micro-manage everything.*

Sonja: *I don't micro-manage everything!*

Richard: *You do! From the font I choose to the margins of the document. Remember when I stayed in the office late to help you do the mock-up for the Backhouse proposal? I was…*

Sonja: *You're the one who's so particular about the unimportant details …*

 It can sometimes be difficult to manage a conflict effectively when the conversation turns into a slinging match where both parties try to gain an advantage and attack each other.

Below are some of the things that Richard and Sonja did in their conversation above that can be unhelpful when trying to resolve a conflict. How many did you spot?

 ## Ten Dos and Don'ts when communicating in a conflict situation

❶ Don't start with a lot of negativity, e.g. *'I have a real issue with the fact that you …'* Instead, consider opening with something positive and showing your appreciation for something that person has done. If possible, try to find opportunities to say positive things throughout the conversation. There is of course the danger that sugar-coating the negatives might come across as being insincere (see ➙ the Hamburger Approach in Chapter 5, page 124), so make sure that the positives you mention are genuine and of value.

❷ Don't make generalisations and over-globalise the issue, e.g. *You always do this …; You never ….; You do this all the time …* Instead, focus on the issue at hand.

❸ Don't present feelings as facts, e.g. *Don't be fake; It's dishonest; You micromanage everything; You pick fault at everything I do.* Instead, use phrases like *It makes me feel …; It seems to me that …; I feel like you …* and be clear when it's your feelings and your presumptions that you're presenting.

❹ Don't bring up past examples that aren't relevant to the issue, e.g. *'Remember when I …'.* Instead, use examples to illustrate what you are saying, but avoid dwelling on too many irrelevant examples. Focus on the overall goal.

❺ Avoid using emotional words and adverbs, e.g. *That's so not true; It's extremely difficult to work with you; That's such rubbish.* Instead, try to manage the negative emotions that arise during a conflict, be aware of your default tendencies and, as far as possible, try to stick to the facts.

❻ Don't focus on insulting their personalities, e.g. *Don't be fake; It's dishonest; You're a control freak; You're always so negative.* Instead, focus on events and behaviours.

❼ Don't get defensive and retaliate, e.g. *I don't … You are the one who's …; Whenever I try to help, you pick fault at everything I do.* Instead, first consider the validity of what is being said and why that person feels that way.

8 Don't interrupt. Instead, let the other party finish what they have to say before formulating your response.

9 Don't ignore what is being said. We are sometimes so keen to defend ourselves and refute what the other has said that we are not really able to process the underlying issue: that our behaviour has caused the other to feel a certain way. Instead, by acknowledging the feelings in the other, we can move on to finding a way of adjusting our behaviour to resolve the situation.

10 Don't focus solely on the past. In an argument, many of us end up becoming fixated on the events of the past. Expressions like, *You should have ...; You could have...* are good hindsights for reflection, but carry elements of blame and one-upmanship. Instead, focus on the future and explore options whereby both parties can move forward. e.g. *In the future, could we try to...; From now on, how about we...?; If it happens again, do you think you could...?*

Now consider the following conversation between Sonja and Richard. Try to notice elements of the above ten tips in the dialogue and how that helps to resolve the conflict.

Sonja: *Richard, I know you try to be helpful and you've said on many occasions that I can turn to you when I feel overwhelmed. I really appreciate that and have taken that to heart, so I felt a bit disappointed when I asked you to help me with the social media report and you seemed reluctant. I only asked you because I know you're very good at navigating social media platforms.*

Richard: *I'm sorry I disappointed you. I really would like to help you, Sonja, but I sometimes find it difficult when I try to help because you seem to know exactly what you want and perhaps you prefer to have better control over the finer details. So I feel like my work often goes to waste when you come in and change what I've worked on.*

Sonja: *I can see how that can make you feel like your efforts have gone to waste. I'm sorry you feel that way. Would it help you in the future if I am clearer from the beginning which elements I would like to have a say in?*

Richard: *Yes, definitely. And I'd like you to trust my expertise a bit more.*

Sonja: *I do. That's why I like you helping me out because you're good at what you do.*

> In the revised dialogue above, Sonja and Richard were better able to identify the areas that were causing a problem in their working relationship, the causes behind them and ways they could move forward. Both of them came away feeling like they had been listened to and that their feelings were acknowledged. Although communicating in conflict situations can be difficult, successful resolutions can be found without damaging the good will between the parties involved. If conducted effectively, it can instead serve to develop the trust and rapport built in the relationships.

Cultural influences in conflict management

When communicating internationally, the chances of misunderstandings and conflict are likely to rise due to vast differences in values and beliefs, working styles, perceptions, and even language use. This is potentially made worse by the increase in virtual teams and the decline in face-to-face communication, both of which are key aspects of global co-operation.

Whether you are a manager of a cross-cultural team, a participant in a global project, working with clients or suppliers across time zones or dealing with superiors who are on a different continent, the ability to adapt and shift our conflict management strategies can be enhanced by an awareness of how conflict tends to be dealt with in different cultures.

Using the Thomas-Kilmann framework of the five conflict management modes as a basis (see ➡ page 149), multiple cross-cultural researchers have considered the impact of culture on preferred styles of conflict management, exploring the possibility of how some styles might be more dominant due to the influence of certain cultural dimensions. While some studies looked at the differences between Eastern and Western preferences[47], others maintain that it would be difficult to generalise as not all East Asians are similar in their

---

47 Most such studies tend to compare participants in countries in East Asia to Americans or Australians. Examples of such studies include:
- Ting-Toomey S (1988) Intercultural communication styles: A face-negotiation theory. In YY Kim and WB Gudykunst (Eds.) *Theories in Intercultural Communication*. Sage: pp213-235
- Lee HO & Rogan RG (1991) A cross-cultural comparison of organizational conflict management. *International Journal of Conflict Management* 2 pp181–199.
- Brew FP & Cairn DR (1993) Styles of managing interpersonal workplace conflict in relation to status and face concern: A study with Anglos and Chinese. *International Journal of Conflict Management* 15 27–56.

conflict management styles[48]. Even within the same country there are bound to be differences in the way individuals deal with conflict, which are in turn influenced by their personalities, their awareness of the context, their ability to deal with negative emotions and manage rapport, and their capacity to be flexible in different situations.

The following aspects and examples should therefore serve as additional knowledge of how culture could potentially influence the preferred conflict management style of an individual.

 Which of these people do you recognise? How would you respond to someone who deals with conflict in a very different way from you?

A   Individualism vs collectivism

Oliver sees himself as an independent person responsible for his own actions. In a conflict situation, he finds it important to be open and honest about his feelings, his concerns, his individual interests and his objectives. He believes that by confronting an issue we are on our way to finding a satisfactory plan of action to resolve it. Oliver sees being assertive as part of knowing who you are and what you want, and believes that those who avoid issues are lacking the confidence to solve the problem. He finds it frustrating dealing with people who are unable to be upfront about what they really want.

Meifu sees himself as part of a team, which is in turn part of his community. His actions and behaviour reflect on the other members of his community and will have an impact on them. Meifu is concerned about how the others in his community see him and what they might say about him. Face is important to him and so he does not like dealing with conflicts in front of others. When possible, he prefers to accommodate or avoid the issue because he does not want to embarrass the other party, make them feel bad or create a scene. He would prefer a win-win scenario, but this must be attained in a way that means everyone can save face.

---

48 Kim TY et al (2007) Conflict management styles: the differences among the Chinese, Japanese and Koreans. In *International Journal of Conflict Management,* 18 (1) pp23–41. See https://doi.org/10.1108/10444060710759309 (accessed September 2018).

B Low power distance vs high power distance

Ida is used to a flat hierarchy where managers are there to organise processes but not to dictate how things should happen. Being cynical of people in authority, she is used to challenging her superiors and disagreeing with them openly. She believes that no one should dominate in a conflict and that having an honest and open dialogue can help all parties understand each other better. Even when managing a conflict with her subordinates, Ida tries to be tactful and is happy to compromise or accommodate.

Vani has great respect for her managers and those in authority and relies on them for instruction and guidance. Challenging and disagreeing with those in power can be seen as disrespectful and have negative consequences. So if Vani has any issues with her superiors, she prefers to either ignore it or accommodate where possible. However, when it comes to Vani's subordinates, Vani is a lot more direct and is happy to confront issues. She expects her subordinates to resolve conflict by taking on board her criticism and her advice.

C Task orientation vs relationship orientation

Jacob wants to get the job done and he wants it to be done well. When there is a conflict, he sees it as an obstacle that is in the way of task progress, and therefore should be dealt with efficiently. In cases where he strongly believes he has the best way of moving forward, he might assert his views and urge the other party to accommodate. He is happy to collaborate on bigger issues but this can take up too much time, and sometimes it might be quicker to simply compromise. Jacob feels that workplace conflicts should be resolved in the workplace. He prefers not to talk about the conflict when he is out having drinks with the other party.

Bruno believes that relationships are the foundations of all good business and likes to spend time cultivating them. When conflict arises, he is keen to resolve it in a way that does not damage the trust and good will he has built up. He might choose to ignore the issue if it isn't substantial, or compromise when possible. After all, overt disagreements can damage relationships. However, when dealing with someone he knows well, he likes to use an accommodation style that promotes an amicable and open discussion, preferably in a restaurant or over drinks after work. However, if Bruno has an issue with a stranger (e.g. the sales assistant in a shop) he would not hesitate to confront them in a more assertive way as he does not fear jeopardising their relationship.

D Long-term vs short-term orientation

Lu tends to look at the big picture and sees how things might be affected in the longer term. She therefore does not feel the need to resolve things immediately as she believes that sometimes by waiting things out, more might come to light. She tends to use the Avoidance Mode when it comes to conflicts but she doesn't see it as avoiding the issues at hand. Akin to a more holistic approach, she believes that there might be a resolution in the long term that cannot be realised immediately. Confronting an issue without proper preparation and understanding of the situation can lead to undesirable consequences. Lu also feels that she can learn lessons from conflict situations without confronting them head-on.

Valentina likes to deal with things promptly and immediately and this might mean confronting the issue on the spot and asserting her point of view. She believes that leaving problems to fester will result in bigger problems in the future. Valentina is happy to engage in an open discussion in a collaborative fashion if this can lead to a tangible solution where objectives are met.

E The role of apologies

Martin was confronted by his manager with a mistake his team had made. In a dialogue to resolve the issue, Martin discussed ways they could fix the problem and move forward, but took great care not to apologise for the mistake. Martin believed that saying sorry would be an admittance of guilt and this would increase the risk of him being blamed for the problem.

Kazu realised that his team had made a mistake and sought to address the issue with his manager. He immediately apologised for the mistake and said he was deeply sorry for what had happened. Kazu believed that he was apologising as a representative of the team and felt that the apology signaled his regret and demonstrated his understanding that this mistake will now cost his manager much time and money to repair. By apologising, Kazu hopes to maintain the relationship his team has with upper management.

F The role of silence

Joyce is not keen on confrontation and does not like to argue. When confronted, she tends to go quiet. She believes that silence is a sign of humility and respect, especially when confronted by superiors or someone in authority, and silence shows the other party that she is listening and taking in what is being said. When Joyce is in conflict resolution talks with someone who speaks a lot, she feels like they are being self-centred and unwilling to learn from the conversation.

Lina likes to see herself as candid, straightforward and honest. She's not afraid of confrontations and believes that the best way to resolve issues is to talk about them openly and collaboratively. She finds people who remain silent during such discussions disrespectful and evasive, and does not think they contribute much to managing the conflict.

Did you find some of the motivations for the above examples familiar? Having a better understanding of the influences that might affect differing conflict management styles can help us avoid making quick judgments and jumping to the wrong conclusions about the way someone chooses to deal with conflict.

The multi-faceted view of conflict

We must remember that conflicts are complex, context-dependent and multi-dimensional, and it would be a mistake to over generalise cultural influences in dealing with conflict.

We must also take into account individual differences when dealing with conflict. While some might prefer to tackle conflict head on and articulate how they feel, others might do anything to avoid confrontation. Personality factors like introversion and extroversion can have an effect on how one approaches conflict situations. Those who have received training in the area of conflict management might also deal with conflict differently, embracing the fact that it can sometimes be better to tactfully acknowledge and confront an issue than to avoid it and let it build up into a bigger one.

An awareness of these varied factors can help prepare us for when there is a stark difference in conflict management style and remind us of the importance of flexibility when trying to navigate this multi-faceted and sensitive area of communication.

Chapter 10: Communicating beyond words

Body language

A lot of communication happens beyond the words we say, and the way we interpret this kind of communication can sometimes be so ingrained within us that it can be hard to change such deep-rooted associations. In both of the situations we're about to look at, we see that it can sometimes be extremely difficult to adapt.

Rose was preparing for her first visit to Japan where she was to meet the top executives of the Japanese branch of her company. She learnt through an online search that the Japanese greeted each other by bowing and that the depth of the bow corresponded with the amount of respect one was showing the other. She also learnt that the Japanese gave and received gifts with both hands, and the same etiquette applies to business cards, which should then be studied carefully and, if possible, placed on the table in front of the receiver. Rose felt prepared but when the time came to greet the Japanese executives, she found herself freezing and unable to return the bow she was given. She managed a nod and give an awkward smile but simply could not bring herself to bow.

Dave recommended his Saudi counterpart, Omar, for a leading role on a project, and Omar was keen to thank Dave when he found out that they would both be at the same conference. They met up during a coffee break and spoke candidly about their work, but throughout the conversation Dave found that Omar kept moving closer to him and Dave would step back, trying to keep what he felt was an appropriate distance. Finally, Dave remarked that it was time for him to go to the next session. Omar offered to walk with him and casually picked up Dave's hand and started to walk hand in hand with Dave. Although Dave knew from his work in the Middle East that Arab men tended to be high on contact (with other men) and that this was Omar's sign of friendship and trust, he found it uncomfortable and had to make an excuse to break off their handholding.

In the above critical incidents, both Rose and Dave had knowledge of the culture they were dealing with and were keen to adapt and make a good impression. However, the bowing (in Rose's case) and the close proximity and handholding (in Dave's case) were a step too far outside their comfort zones and they found themselves unable to get past their own behavioural conditioning. Rose had a deep-seated belief that bowing represented submission and was unable to relinquish that association when it came to the time for her to bow. For Dave, close proximity and handholding represented a kind of intimacy which he usually reserved for his wife, and his instinctive response to anyone trying to get as close was to move away.

Although Rose and Dave had difficulty adapting, they were aware of the issues underlying those challenges. They were open to acquiring knowledge about the other culture's way of doing things, and they were willing to try to adapt. When they were unable to, they were able to reflect on the reasons why and were aware of their reactions and the possible impact on their interactions. One could therefore say that half their battle had been won. If necessary, with practice and more exposure, Rose and Dave could re-condition themselves to successfully adapt to these new ways.

Cross-cultural non-verbal communication

In this chapter, we will be looking at how different uses of non-verbal communication can have different cultural associations and be interpreted differently. As this is not a cultural dictionary and therefore not a comprehensive list of cross-cultural practices, the observations mentioned here serve as a starting point for the things you could consider when communicating internationally. Some of these practices might be fairly easy to adapt to, while others might require practice and increased exposure.

Look at the eight scenarios below and pick the answer you think most applies to you. Note that there are no absolute right or wrong answers.

1   You are working at a bar and a customer comes up and asks for beers in a foreign language you don't understand. He gestures using his thumb and index finger and you understand the word 'beer'. How many beers do you serve him?

(a)   Two beers.

(b)   Seven beers.

(c)   None. You interpret his behaviour as aggressive and call for your manager.

2   You are chairing a meeting for the first time and from the back of the room your colleague gestures towards you with a thumbs-up. What do you think he's trying to say to you?

(a)   This is going well!

(b)   Here's a rude gesture to tell you what I think of you!

(c)   Look up!

3   You are giving a presentation to a group of 50. As you look out into the sea of people, everyone has the most serious of faces and not a single smile is in sight. You think this must be because...

(a)   They don't like your presentation.

(b)   They are very serious people.

(c)   They want to show you and the event respect.

4   You want to change the location of the next meeting and are trying to find out if your colleague agrees with this. He tilts his head from side to side in what is best described as a head bobble. What does he mean?

(a)   He agrees with this.

(b)   He doesn't agree with this.

(c)   He isn't sure about this.

5   Your boss is reprimanding you for something you have done. Do you...

(a)   Look at him in the eye?

(b)   Look at his nose or other parts of his face?

(c)   Look down at the ground?

6   **You are at a job interview. How would you sit?**

(a)   With your legs wide open, knees far apart, with your back relaxed against the back of the chair.

(b)   Sitting upright, with your legs neatly crossed (the back of your knee resting on your other knee).

(c)   With your legs crossed in a figure four (your calf or ankle resting on the knee of the other leg).

(d)   Sitting upright, with your legs parallel to each other.

7   **You are talking to a business acquaintance and they stand close enough for you to smell their breath. You think they are...**

(a)   Too close for comfort.

(b)   Being polite and involved in the relationship you both are nurturing.

(c)   Sexually attracted to you.

8   **During a social occasion, your manager joins your group conversation by resting their arm casually on your shoulder for a few seconds. You feel...**

(a)   Uncomfortable because you don't like being touched.

(b)   Happy because they clearly like you.

(c)   Strange because you think this means they might be flirting with you.

 Now go back and look at the alternative answers to each question. Are you aware of which national cultures those alternatives might apply to? What might the impact be of communicating with someone who picked those alternatives?

Now read the following explanations. Which ones were you already familiar with?

1   Gesturing by sticking out your thumb and index finger signals the number 2 in Germany but the number 7 in China. In some Western countries, that hand gesture is also used to represent a gun.

2   Although the thumbs-up says 'good' or 'well done' in many countries, it could be a rude gesture in the Middle East, Bangladesh, Greece and several other regions. Pointing with your index finger is considered rude in some parts of the

---

world. For the ethnic Malays in Malaysia, pointing with the thumb in place of the index finger is not uncommon and might be the norm for some.

3   In countries like the US and the UK, we often use smiles to break the ice, to convey friendliness and to show respect and openness. In a presentation, the Americans and the British might rely on the smiles of the audience to put them at ease and make them feel welcome. However, casual smiling is not encouraged in some societies. A Russian proverb even states that 'a *smile without reason is a sign of idiocy*' and a so-called 'smile of respect' is seen as insincere and often regarded with suspicion in Russia. From a young age, Russian children are taught to look serious in class so as to treat the lesson with the appropriate respect.

In a piece of research[1] done on smiles across cultures, the researchers found that smiling individuals were considered more intelligent than non-smiling people in countries such as Germany, Switzerland, China and Malaysia. However, in countries like Russia, Japan, South Korea and Iran, the smiling faces were rated as less intelligent than the non-smiling ones. Meanwhile, in countries like India, Argentina and the Maldives, smiling was associated with dishonesty.

4   The head bobble means 'good', 'yes', 'I understand', or 'okay' in India. In the western world, we often use the head nod to mean the same thing, but in countries like Bulgaria and Albania, the vertical nod of the head might mean 'no'.

5   In countries like the US, Australia, the UK, and most parts of Europe, maintaining eye contact with someone is often a way of showing that you are paying attention and that you are interested in what they are saying. In contrast, direct eye contact is not as common in many parts of Asia, where one might instead look at other parts of the face or neck so as to be polite. When speaking to a superior, many Japanese and Koreans prefer to look down as a sign of respect as eye contact might be interpreted as challenging what is being said. In parts of South America and Africa, prolonged eye contact could also be seen as challenging authority. Meanwhile, in the Middle East, eye contact across genders is considered inappropriate, although eye contact within a gender could signify honesty and truthfulness.

1   Krys K, Melanie Vauclair C, Capaldi CA *et al* (2016) Be careful when you smile: culture shapes judgments of intelligence and honesty of smiling individuals. *Journal of Nonverbal Behaviour* **40** 2 pp101–116.

6   Your posture and the way you sit can say a lot about you, and this can depend not only on national cultures, but also on your gender, the corporate culture and the social context. To some, a man sitting with his legs wide open and his back relaxed against the chair might signal a relaxed confidence and openness, while to others, the very same sitting position might convey disrespect, arrogance and even vulgarity.

Sitting cross-legged in front of your superiors could be considered rude in countries like Japan and Korea, and the display of the bottoms of your feet or your shoes in the figure-four crossed-legged position might offend people in the Middle East. Sitting upright with legs parallel to each other seems to be a neutral position that signals respect and an appropriate level of seriousness.

7   Many of us have an instinctive preference for how close we'd like our conversation partners to stand. While we're more likely to tolerate a closer distance with family and close friends, this distance might widen when talking to acquaintances and colleagues. The study of such physical proximity and the way we use space is called 'proxemics' and it has been discovered that different cultures might have a different perception of what that appropriate distance might be. People from the US, Canada, the UK and the Nordic countries might have a need for more personal space, sometimes standing at arms' length when having a conversation with a colleague, whereas people from South America, the Middle East and some parts of Europe might be more comfortable standing closer, as it might signify being more involved.

8   We can also see proxemics at play when observing the personal space needed in public situations e.g. when queuing among strangers. While the Chinese, the Indians and the Koreans might be comfortable brushing against strangers in a queue, the British and the Japanese tend to keep a certain distance from the person in front. Gender also plays a part, especially in the Middle East, where contact between genders might be frowned upon.

Closely related to the study of proxemics is the study of haptics – how touch is used in communication. People from countries like France, Turkey, Italy, Greece and India might be more comfortable with touching someone socially to convey concern,

> gratitude, sympathy or friendship. Meanwhile, touching is confined to handshakes and perhaps a friendly slap on the back in countries like the US or the UK, and social touching in some Asian countries like Japan and Korea is more uncommon. Again, we need to consider the role of gender, since touching within the same gender might be very common in the Middle East but inappropriate across genders.

A holistic approach to interpreting body language

When considering different aspects of body language, as with other aspects of intercultural communication, we need to be careful not to over-generalise. Communication is highly dependent on context and the people involved are individuals capable of flexibility and change, and will often defy stereotypes. When interpreting someone's body language, it is important to take into consideration how it matches with the other communicative messages they are sending: e.g. the words they are saying, their facial expression, their stance, etc. before jumping to any conclusions.

It is also important to reflect on the values and beliefs that underline the behaviour or attitudes that are different from your own, e.g. using the DIE model (see ➜ 'Dealing with intercultural communication' on page 43), so as to help us better understand and better deal with the differences in the way we communicate.

Paralanguage: it's not what you say, it's how you say it

When I first arrived in the UK many years ago, I lived in a houseshare with eight British working adults and found myself taking the rubbish in the kitchen bin out to the communal bin nearly every day. Speaking with a Singaporean accent, I decided to ask my housemates for help, saying, 'Could you take the bins OUT, PLEASE?' (Note words are deliberately capitalised to signal word stress.)

I overheard them talking about me the next day, referring to me as rude and abrupt. So the next time I asked them for help with the bins, I used a more polite request, 'I was wondering if you could take the bins OUT, PLEASE.' But, it turned out that changing my words did not have any effect on their impression of me. I was puzzled and couldn't understand why.

On a different occasion, a British friend said something similar to me, and went on to explain that it was perhaps due to the staccato rhythm and the fast speed of my speech that made me come across abrupt. I was disturbed by how my character was being judged according to the rhythm and tempo of the way I spoke, and began to adapt to the environment I was in by gradually adjusting the paralinguistic features of my speech in order to avoid any future misunderstandings.

Years later, I came across the work of Interactional Sociolinguist John J Gumperz and his findings[49] in London in the 1970s. Heathrow Airport had hired a group of Indian and Pakistani women to serve the baggage handlers at the staff cafeteria, but the baggage handlers found their new servers rude and the female servers complained of discrimination. Conflict ensued and Gumperz was called in to pinpoint the source of the problem. He observed that it all came down to the intonation of one word, *'gravy'*. The British women would offer the baggage handlers gravy by asking the one-word question, *'Gravy?'*, with an upward intonation, while their Indian and Pakistani counterparts would use the same word but with a downward intonation. To the British baggage handlers, the rising intonation suggested a polite offer, like, *'Would you like some gravy?'* The falling intonation, which was more characteristic of the Indian and Pakistani accent in English, represented a statement to the British workers, making the one-word question sound like a rude, *'Here's the gravy — if you want it, take it!'*

Such misjudgments of the speakers' intention can take place solely due to the way someone speaks and the paralinguistic features (a.k.a. paralanguage) they employ, i.e. their pitch, intonation, speed, range of tones, rhythm, tempo, etc. The Japanese and some Middle-Eastern cultures might, for example, interpret speech with a wider range of intonation as feminine or child-like, while the British and Americans might interpret a more monotonous speech pattern as boring and lacking in dynamism. The way we interpret someone's use of paralanguage can sometimes be so ingrained within us that we might not even be conscious of it. When we are made aware of the differences in interpretation, we can then better understand the source of our miscommunication and avoid any further misunderstandings.

---

49 Gumperz JJ (1982) *Discourse Strategies*. Cambridge: Cambridge University Press.

Look at the dialogue below.
What do you think is the source of this miscommunication?

Amelia has just come back to the office from a short trip abroad and is talking to her colleague, Minwoo...

Amelia: *You won't believe what happened to me at the airport.* (Minwoo looks in her direction but doesn't say a word.)

Amelia: *You know how they don't allow you on some flights with an overhead cabin bag unless you pay extra?* (She looks to Minwoo and Minwoo looks back in intense silence.)

Amelia: *So I paid for that upgrade when I was checking in, right? But when I got to the boarding gate, they said they had no record of my upgrade! And they took my bag off me!* (Minwoo continues to look in her direction in silence.)

Amelia: *Look, if you're not interested in my story, it's fine. Forget about it.*

In the conversation above, Amelia was expecting some backchanelling from Minwoo, i.e. utterances and sounds to show interest and demonstrate that he was actively listening e.g. *Uh-huh; Hmm-mm; Yah?; Really?; No way!*. In contrast, Minwoo, who comes from a South Korean background, sees backchanelling as interrupting the speaker and prefers to demonstrate respect and attentive listening by remaining silent.

Backchannelling is used in many cultures but this can vary in frequency and purpose. The Japanese, for example, tend to use such high levels of backchannelling[1] that they even have the word *Aizuchi'* to describe these frequent interjections used to acknowledge and show understanding of what the speaker is saying. The mis-interpretation of these interjections can sometimes cause severe miscommunication, as seen in the famous IBM-Hitachi-Mitsubishi trial of the 1980s[2], where Hitachi and Mitsubishi were alleged to have tried to steal secrets from IBM. Based on his use of Aizuchi[3], Mr Ishida, an employee of Mitsubishi, was accused by the FBI of being a company spy because his interjecting noises were mistakenly interpreted as signalling agreement when he had intended to signal understanding.

---

1 For more research on this, see: https://ir.uiowa.edu/cgi/viewcontent.cgi?article=3464&context=etd (accessed September 2018).

2 For more on this case: https://www.nytimes.com/1983/11/05/business/the-publicity-effect-of-ibm-sting.html (accessed September 2018).

3 LoCastro V (1987) Aizuchi: A Japanese conversational routine. In LE Smith (Ed) *Discourse Across Cultures: Strategies in World Englishes* (pp101–113). New York: Prentice Hall.

For someone used to a more active way of participating in a conversation, silence can be daunting and disconcerting. However, silence can take on many meanings and be interpreted in a variety of ways. For some, silence in a conversation can mean boredom and a lack of interest, whereas for others, silence might signal thinking time or deference. In some cultures, silence is consent while in others, silence means, 'No, but I'm too polite to say it'. It is therefore important to clarify what someone means before making assumptions.

Other customs and practices

Aside from our body language and paralanguage, our rituals, our habits and our practices can be a huge part of how we communicate with others. An ignorance of such practices could sometimes be misinterpreted as disrespectful or even offensive.

Consider the following scenarios and, on a scale of 1 to 3, rate how polite or rude you think this behaviour might be.

1 = polite   2 = neither rude nor polite   3 = rude.

1	You are a high-level executive and in a meeting with the CEO of your client company. You realise that he's dressed in a T-shirt and jeans.	
2	On a visit to China you are invited to a Chinese restaurant by your Chinese counterpart and his team. The moment you arrive, you sit yourself down on the nearest chair by the door.	
3	In the middle of the meal, Javier sticks his chopsticks vertically into his rice bowl while he takes a break from his food.	
4	While having drinks with you and some colleagues, Elaine realises that her glass is empty and so she reaches out for the bottle to give herself a re-fill, before replacing the bottle.	
5	When it's time to get the bill, Vicky seeks to split the total equally with you and your fellow diners.	

6	You are giving a presentation and the people in the room are talking as you talk.	
7	You invite your colleague to your house for dinner and they take their shoes off at the front door.	
8	You go out for drinks with two other colleagues, Arthur and Alfred. You pay for the first round of drinks for everyone and then Arthur pays for a second round of drinks. When Alfred finishes his second drink, he thanks you and Arthur for the drinks, and leaves.	
9	You pay a visit to your supplier and bring a gift wrapped in beautiful paper. Your supplier thanks you for the gift and unwraps it on the spot.	
10	You are in a meeting and your colleague Sandy blows her nose.	

Did you find yourself reacting strongly to any of the above? While you might find some of the characters in the above scenarios extremely rude and disrespectful, you might also see nothing wrong with others. Look at the scenarios again and consider the underlying attitudes and beliefs that might have given rise to your reactions. Now read the explanations below. Were you aware of these cultural faux pas? How might this knowledge affect your behaviour in such situations?

1   Dress codes can vary from company to company and culture to culture. You can be sure to expect a different attitude to workwear when in a meeting with someone from Apple as opposed to someone from HSBC. Even within the same company, dress codes can differ depending on the workplace settings. Employees from the IT department or the warehousing department might dress differently from those in the sales and marketing department. Some people have noticed that the Japanese executives tend to dress more formally than some American executives. So if you are going to be in an important meeting with someone you have never met, take into consideration the dress code of their corporation, their community and their culture. If you have a flexible dress code, you might want to consider adapting.

2   When doing business in China, you will often find yourself being taken out to dinner with a team of colleagues with the goal of building trust and relationships. In formal dinners, the seating arrangement can be extremely important, and there can be many unspoken rules about the seating arrangements at different types of tables.

A general rule of thumb to follow is that the most important person, i.e. the guest of honour, should sit facing the entrance, with those of the highest positions to their left and right. The least important person sits closest to the door, so that they are able to liaise with the serving staff. If you are unsure of where to sit let your host guide you. Remember that if you are not the guest of honour, stay standing until the guest sits.

3   Most East Asian countries that use chopsticks consider it a taboo to stick chopsticks vertically into a rice bowl. For the Japanese and Koreans, this resembles a funeral rite while for the Chinese and the Vietnamese it looks like incense sticks used for prayer and offerings. Instead, when taking a break, place the chopsticks beside the bowl on the table.

4   In Western communities it is often considered good etiquette to look around the table to see who needs a refill and offer to pour them a drink before pouring yourself one. In Japan and Korea, some people frown upon pouring your own drink. Instead, offer to pour your drinking partners a drink, and then they'll pour you one as a sign of mutual respect.

5   How a bill is split can often depend on the occasion, the age of those involved and the culture. Some groups tend to split the bill equally regardless of what was ordered, and some prefer to just pay for what they ate/drank. In some cultures, the person who has done the inviting or hosting takes care of the whole bill, while in others, the oldest person in the group does the paying. If you are the guest, it might help to wait and see what the norm of the group might be and offer to pay even if someone insists on paying the bill.

6   While some of us might expect total silence and undivided attention when we are speaking, others from a more flexible-time culture (see → 'Cultural frameworks and dimensions' on page 33) might be used to multi-tasking and having different things draw

on their attention at the same time. In Janet Holmes's study[1] on politeness in intercultural communication, she found that in the Māori culture it is in fact a sign of respect for people to talk about what you are saying as you are saying it, and this background chatter demonstrates support, engagement and approval of the speaker.

7   In many countries in Asia, parts of Europe (Finland, Sweden, Germany, Ukraine, etc.), and in many Muslim cultures, it is socially unacceptable to wear shoes that are used outdoors in the house. This is mainly for cleanliness and hygiene purposes, and is especially common in cultures where people tend to sit on the floor. Some also see the removing of shoes as symbolising respect for the act of stepping into one's private space. Be careful when leaving the house not to bring the shoes in when you put them back on!

8   In some communities, the more senior or the more wealthy members of the group tend to buy the drinks for everyone, and in others it is common for the individuals to buy and pay for their own drinks. However, in countries like Ireland, Australia, New Zealand, Canada and the UK, the culture of 'buying rounds' is very much the norm. This involves taking turns to buy drinks for the group and it is considered impolite to avoid your turn, especially when you have benefitted from the drinks other people have bought you. If you know you have to leave early, consider buying an earlier round. Alternatively, when it comes to your turn and you really can't stay for another round of drinks, offer to buy the others their next drinks but leave yourself out.

9   Gift-giving can be a bit of a minefield if you don't know what to expect. In some cultures, e.g. Japan, it is standard to bring gifts when visiting an office or when coming back to your office from a trip abroad while in other cultures, e.g. the UK, this might not be expected.

When to open the gift can vary: in some communities it is considered rude not to open the gift in front of the giver and give them the pleasure of enjoying your reaction to the gift. In contrast, others might consider it rude and you might even risk embarrassing the giver by opening the gift in front of them as it might look like you are placing importance on the material quality of the gift and not the generous act of giving itself.

1   Holmes J (2012) Politeness in intercultural discourse and communication. In: CB Paulston (Ed) *The Handbook of Intercultural Discourse and Communication*. Oxford: Blackwell Publishing. pp205-228.

> What to give is also problematic - too expensive a gift could be mistaken for bribery while too cheap a gift could be seen as an insult. It might be worth researching the gift-giving habits of your counterparts before meeting them, and try to reciprocate if you've been given a gift.
>
> 10 Although some people think of blowing one's nose as a natural bodily function and do not have an issue with it being done in public, there are others who find the act disgusting. If you want to play it safe, especially when you are in countries like Japan or France, leave the room when you need to blow your nose, or do it discreetly into a tissue and make sure that you are nowhere near food.

We can't know everything!

Customs and rules for behaviour can differ widely in different communities and different countries. While it can be useful to find out beforehand the appropriate etiquette for the people we are going to meet and the countries we are going to visit, it is often impossible to be prepared for every situation we might encounter. What we can do is train ourselves to become more sensitive to our conversation partners and to notice incidents where a faux pas has been committed or where miscommunication has taken place. For only when we become aware that intentions have been misinterpreted can we seek to improve the situation: whether we choose to do this by adapting our behaviour, accepting their behaviour, or talking openly about the differences.

Each mistake can be a learning experience, so when faced with behaviour or attitudes that clash with our own, we can use the DIE model to help us reflect on the possible underlying reasons, values and beliefs, and apply the ADAPT model to give us the power and the flexibility to make the changes we need (see → 'Dealing with intercultural communication' on page 43 for more on both the DIE and ADAPT models). And by dealing with our differences pro-actively, we can strive for more successful international communication.

Conclusion

There are many factors that influence the way we communicate: our upbringing, the communities we associate with, our personalities and our individual preferences etc.

Culture plays a big part in how we see the world and how we might choose to operate, but culture isn't black and white and isn't simply related to nationalities or geographical regions. It surpasses stereotypes and generalisations, and although there might be tendencies, those are also fluid depending on the context.

Similarly, we do not have one way of communicating and the ways we communicate are not set in stone. Most of us have a range of communication styles and tools that we employ, and they can vary greatly depending on the people we talk to and the circumstances we are in. We speak to our children differently from the way we speak to our managers. The communication strategies we use at an office party would differ significantly from those we use when dealing with a conflict.

When dealing with international communication, we might initially encounter a certain amount of resistance within ourselves when confronted with someone who sees things or does things in a different way to us. We might be tempted to pass quick judgments and interpret certain behaviours according to the filters we are used to.

Nonetheless, hopefully this book has shown you that it can sometimes be worth taking a moment to reflect on the situation and see it from a different perspective. While reading through the critical incidents and working through the tasks in this book, you might have become more aware of your own tendencies and standpoints, you might have gained an alternative way of looking at things, or you might have been reminded of past situations you have been in yourself.

By constantly reflecting on and increasing our awareness of the way we communicate, we can strive towards more effective and successful international communication. Because we are also flexible creatures capable of adaptation. With a good dose of awareness and critical thinking skills, we can change the way we perceive things and adapt our reactions and behaviour when necessary.

So, when faced with your own version of a critical incident, remember to pause and 'ADAPT':

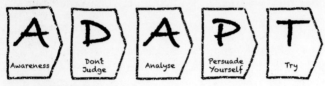

The ADAPT Model

1. be **A**ware of what is happening.

2. **D**on't be too quick to judge.

3. **A**nalyse the situation and the possible interpretations and the values and beliefs that underlie the behaviour.

4. **P**ersuade yourself by finding commonality between your beliefs and your wide range of communication skills.

5. **T**ry doing or seeing things slightly differently from the way you're used to.

Our journey to becoming more successful international communicators continues from here. We can start by collecting our own critical incidents as we communicate across cultures. We can pay attention to the different ways people communicate and ask more questions. We can learn to talk more openly about the way we communicate with each other. We can develop our communication skills by seeking out opportunities to practise them. Lastly, we can enjoy our journey learning all about the differences and similarities in the way we see the world.

Have a good journey and good luck!